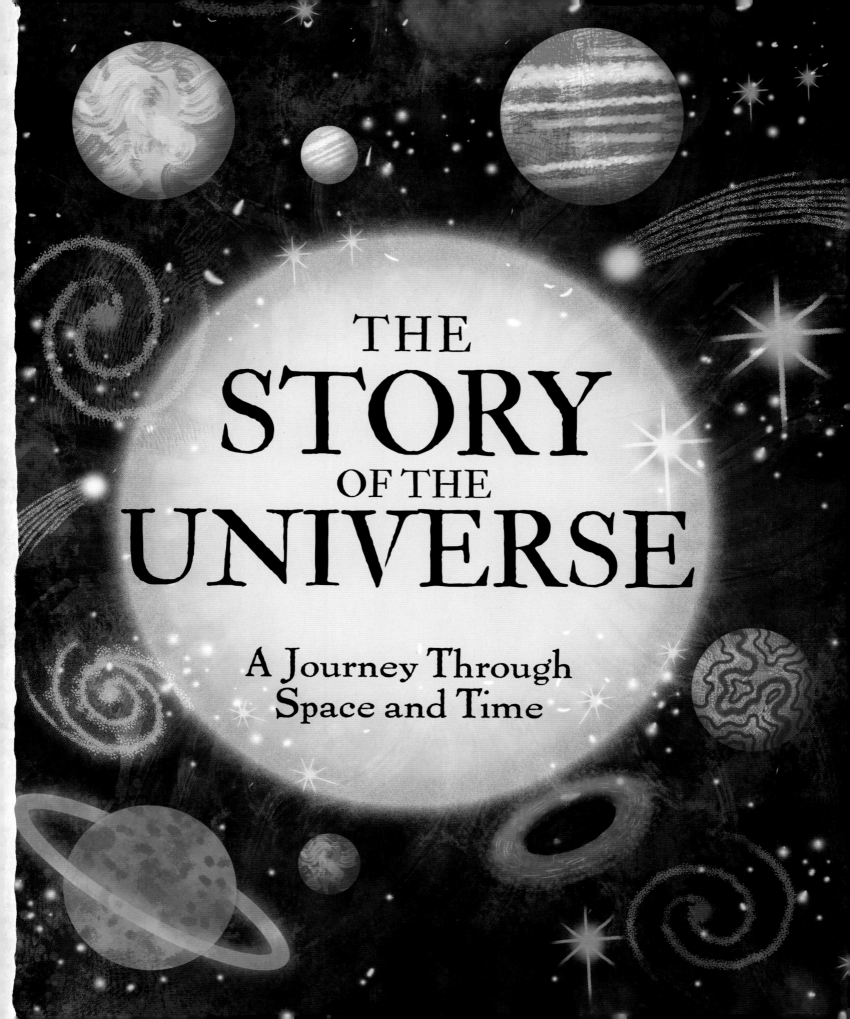

# THE STORY OF THE UNIVERSE

## A Journey Through Space and Time

# THE STORY OF THE UNIVERSE

## A Journey Through Space and Time

By Anne Rooney
Illustrations by Nat Hues

ARCTURUS

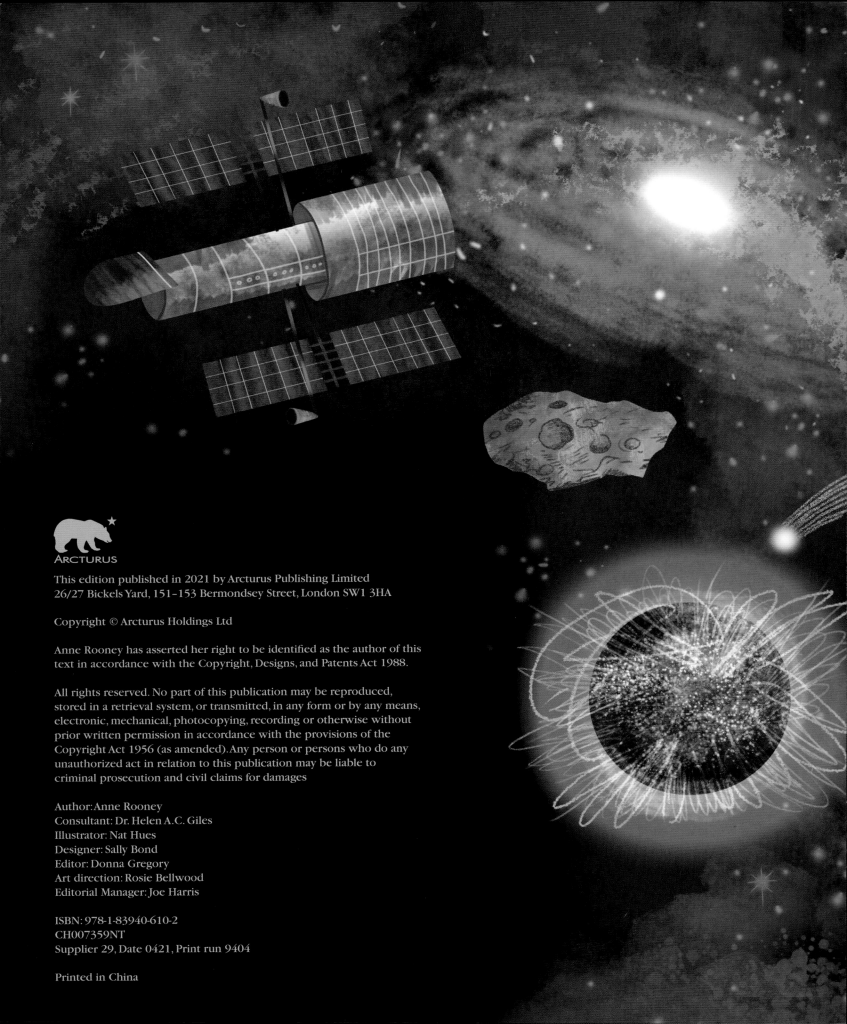

ARCTURUS

This edition published in 2021 by Arcturus Publishing Limited
26/27 Bickels Yard, 151–153 Bermondsey Street, London SW1 3HA

Author: Anne Rooney
Consultant: Dr. Helen A.C. Giles
Illustrator: Nat Hues
Designer: Sally Bond
Editor: Donna Gregory
Art direction: Rosie Bellwood
Editorial Manager: Joe Harris

ISBN: 978-1-83940-610-2
CH007359NT
Supplier 29, Date 0421, Print run 9404

Printed in China

# CONTENTS

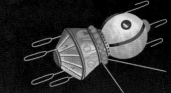

# Introduction

It's the biggest story there is—the story of the entire universe. The universe is all that exists in space and, as far as we know, all that has ever existed in time. It is unimaginably vast, full of wonders and mysteries that have fascinated people for thousands of years.

### Numberless stars

People have always seen the Moon, stars, and planets in the night sky. Long ago, our ancestors could have seen around 5,000 stars on a clear night with a new Moon, but if you live in a modern city you might see just 40. The modern world is so bright that light pollution makes most stars invisible in many places, even on a clear night.

Before the invention of the telescope 400 years ago, people gazed at the dome of sky above them and assumed they could see all there is. But there are far more stars than we can see, even with the most powerful telescopes. Just our own galaxy, the Milky Way, contains hundreds of billions of stars—and there are hundreds of billions of other galaxies.

A **star** shines with its own light; it is a glowing ball of hot dense gases.

A **planet** does not shine, but reflects light from its star. It is a ball of rock, metal, or gas, much cooler than a star.

## The planets and the stars

The Sun and Moon are clearly distinct, but both planets and stars look like tiny points of light in the night sky. They are very different, though. Planets are other worlds going around our own star, the Sun, while stars are other suns far away. People have known there is a difference between planets and stars for thousands of years. They look different—stars twinkle, but planets don't. And the stars all appear to move slowly together in a block but the planets move independently against the background of the stars.

## Where, when, how, and why?

As soon as people began to study the movements of the Moon, planets, and stars they probably wondered what they were, where they came from, and why they are there. Many myths, fables, and religions try to explain the existence of the world and the cosmos. Some myths tell of a "cosmic egg," which is broken apart, one half becoming Earth and everything on it, and the other half becoming the sky and everything in it. Other stories talk of a god creating everything either from nothing or from chaos—a disordered mix of matter.

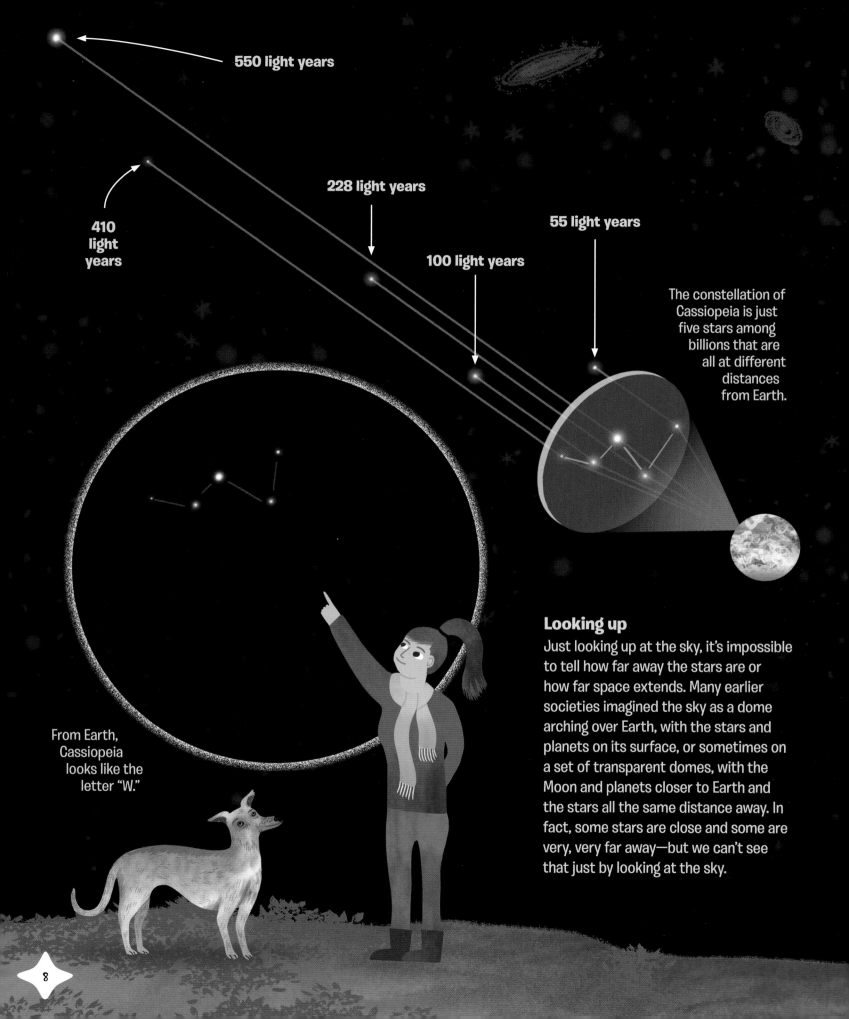

550 light years

410 light years

228 light years

100 light years

55 light years

The constellation of Cassiopeia is just five stars among billions that are all at different distances from Earth.

From Earth, Cassiopeia looks like the letter "W."

## Looking up

Just looking up at the sky, it's impossible to tell how far away the stars are or how far space extends. Many earlier societies imagined the sky as a dome arching over Earth, with the stars and planets on its surface, or sometimes on a set of transparent domes, with the Moon and planets closer to Earth and the stars all the same distance away. In fact, some stars are close and some are very, very far away—but we can't see that just by looking at the sky.

## A scientific story

Today, science helps us explain the universe and how it came about. Science differs from myth and religion in that it collects evidence and suggests an explanation for the way things are, then tests that explanation through experiments and observations. If the explanation doesn't work when tested, it is changed. Over time, science produces a more detailed picture of how things are. Occasionally, a new discovery overturns the explanation completely. Until about 1600 CE, almost everyone assumed that Earth stood still right in the middle of the universe and the Sun, Moon, planets, and stars all went around it. Now we know that Earth and the other planets move around the Sun. It's not possible to observe, just by watching, whether Earth moves in space or whether Earth is still and everything else moves.

**Galileo Galilei**
Italian astronomer
1564–1642

Our understanding of the universe has increased so much that we can now send astronauts up to outer space.

## More mysteries

Hundreds of years ago, people knew much less about the universe and what is in it. We now know a great deal—but we also know that there is a lot that we still don't know! There is plenty still to debate and to discover in our study of the universe. Dive in and find out about the cosmos you live in. Perhaps one day you, too, will become an astronomer and explore the mysteries of the universe.

# IT BEGAN WITH A BANG

Our universe burst into existence in a moment, billions of years ago. In that instant, which scientists call the "Big Bang," space and time both began in an incredibly tiny, hot, dense point. That point was all there was— there was nothing outside it, as it contained all space, and nothing before it, as time began with it.

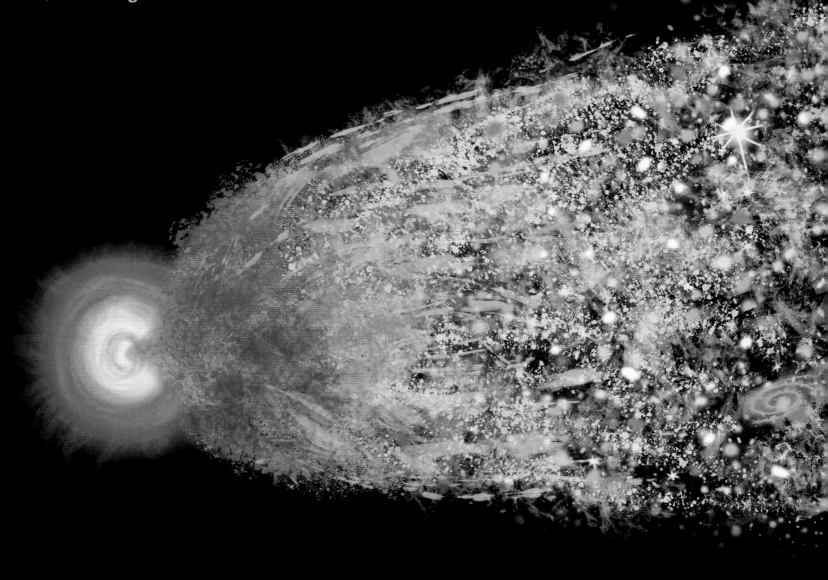

The micro-universe instantly began to grow and change, creating the energy and then the matter that would become go on to become the universe we see around us. It has been getting bigger ever since, and is still getting bigger today. We don't even know how large it is. We can't see to the edge, even with our most powerful telescopes.

# ALL FROM NOTHING

Although the universe started with a "Big Bang," there was no loud bang and it wasn't big! The universe began as a "singularity"—an unimaginably dense, unimaginably tiny point. Everything that is now in the universe came from there, but it was not in any form we would now recognize.

## HOW DO WE KNOW?

We know the Big Bang must have happened because in the 1920s, scientists discovered that the universe is expanding (getting bigger). If it's getting bigger now, then it must have been smaller before. If we go back far enough, the universe must once have been infinitely small—too small to measure or even imagine.

The Big Bang took place billions of years ago. Until recently, scientists thought it happened 13.8 billion years ago, but in 2019, new discoveries suggested it might have been more recent—perhaps just 12.5 billion years ago. Either way, it's been a long, long time.

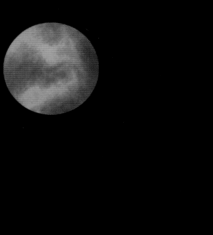

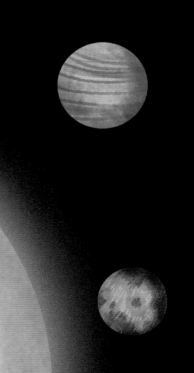

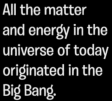

All the matter and energy in the universe of today originated in the Big Bang.

## Feel the force—gravity

In the first tiny fraction of a second, less even than a billionth of a billionth of a second, gravity appeared. Gravity acts between objects that have mass, pulling them together. Gravity holds you firmly on Earth so that you don't float off into space. It holds the Moon in orbit around Earth, and keeps Earth in orbit around the Sun. The first person to explain how gravity keeps objects on Earth and keeps the planets moving around the Sun was the English scientist Isaac Newton, in 1687.

**Isaac Newton**

You could think of gravity as something that changes space-time, the combination of space and time that shapes the universe. If you and a friend hold a blanket taut so that it has a flat surface, then drop a heavy ball onto it, the blanket will dip around the ball. If you add another, lighter ball, it will roll toward the dip. Gravity does exactly this in space. An object with lots of mass, such as a planet or star, makes a big dip, and other objects tend to move toward it. But instead of being in a blanket, the dip is in the three dimensions of space and a fourth dimension of time. What does a dip in time look like? Who knows! But as something gets closer to the dip, time goes more slowly for it.

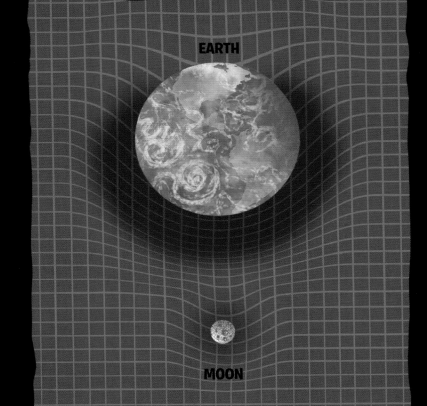

**EARTH**

**MOON**

# AN ENERGY UNIVERSE

The new universe didn't contain any matter—there were no objects. It held only energy. We're used to energy when it's doing things, like making a car move (energy from fuel), or making a light glow (energy from electricity), or even when we're being energetic and moving our bodies (energy from food). It's hard to think of energy on its own, but you need to get your head around energy to understand the universe!

## Energy of all sorts

There are lots of different sorts of energy. The light we can see, called visible light, is a type of energy that moves as waves. It comes in little packets called photons. Lots of other types of energy do this, too. The microwaves that cook your food, the radio waves that carry sound and video, and the X-rays that doctors use to look at broken bones are all types of wave energy. These waves are called "electromagnetic radiation." The universe is full of electromagnetic radiation. It pours from stars and surrounds us.

## WAVY WATER

Waves in the sea might look like moving water, but they are actually energy moving through the water. The water doesn't move from the middle of the sea to the coast. You can see this if you watch something bobbing in the sea—it goes up and down with the waves but isn't carried along far. Each patch of water moves in a circle as the energy of the wave goes through it.

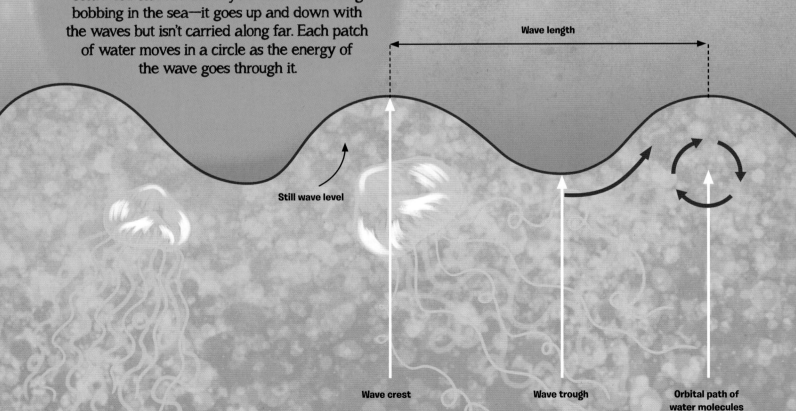

Wave length

Still wave level

Wave crest

Wave trough

Orbital path of water molecules

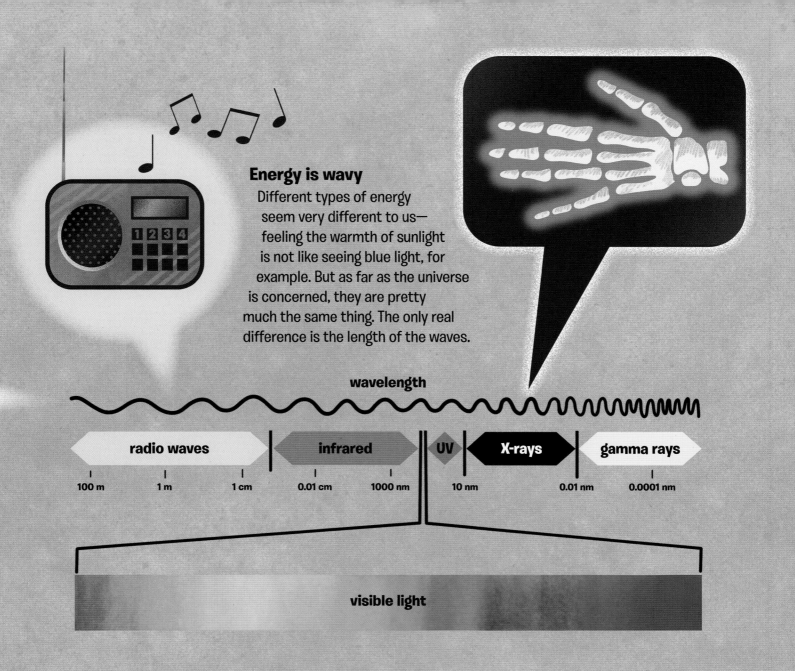

## Energy is wavy

Different types of energy seem very different to us—feeling the warmth of sunlight is not like seeing blue light, for example. But as far as the universe is concerned, they are pretty much the same thing. The only real difference is the length of the waves.

**wavelength**

| radio waves | infrared | UV | X-rays | gamma rays |

| 100 m | 1 m | 1 cm | 0.01 cm | 1000 nm | 10 nm | 0.01 nm | 0.0001 nm |

**visible light**

The distance from the top of one wave to the top of the next is called the wavelength. The radio waves used by a smartphone are a few inches long—up to 42 cm (16.5 in). The wavelength of red light is tiny—635-700 nanometers, or 0.0000635-0.00007 cm (0.000025-0.0000275 in).

All electromagnetic radiation moves at the same speed. This means that the number of waves that can go past a point in one second depends on how long the waves are. For a short wavelength, lots of waves can go by in a second. If the waves are longer, fewer can go by. The number of waves that can go by is called the frequency. A mobile phone works at about 3,000 million waves per second!

# A MEGA-GROWTH SPURT

Early in the first second after the Big Bang, the universe grew almost instantly from being unimaginably small to about the size of a grain of sand, a golf ball, or perhaps a grapefruit. These objects sound quite different, but on the scale of the universe's expansion they are about the same size.

## Bigger and bigger

Scientists aren't quite sure how big the universe ended up, but the rate of growth was mind-blowing. In a hundredth of a billionth of a trillionth of a trillionth of a second, the size of the universe doubled at least 90 times. It became 100,000,000,000,000,000,000,000,000 times its original size. That's a 1 and 26 zeros (which scientists write as $10^{26}$). We call the universe's growth spurt "cosmic inflation."

**COSMIC INFLATION**

## Frozen patterns

When cosmic inflation began, the universe was filled with energy. It was always changing, and the energy was not evenly distributed. This happened on an incredibly tiny scale—the universe was smaller than an atom (see How Big is an Atom, right). But expansion froze the energy state of the universe, almost like taking a snapshot of it.

The pattern of energy in the universe at the moment inflation started was blown up to a massive size. The easiest way to think of it is as rather like a balloon being blown up. If you draw a pattern on a balloon and then blow it up, the things you have drawn get bigger and farther apart as more balloon-surface is added in between them. This is similar to what happened during cosmic inflation.

The frozen pattern made the expanded universe slightly uneven, with some areas having a bit more energy than others. The areas with more energy were warmer. The unevenness was fixed forever. It would eventually lead to the pattern of galaxies the universe has now.

## Still growing

The universe didn't stop growing after cosmic inflation, but its growth continued at a much slower rate. It has since grown to 1,000,000,000,000,000,000,000,000,000,000 ($10^{30}$) times its size at the end of cosmic inflation. That's only 10,000 times more growth over 12–14 billion years than it managed during cosmic inflation. At first, it settled into a steady pattern of growth, but it has since speeded up again. It's now growing faster and faster—but it will never grow as fast as it did in its early growth spurt.

Frozen pattern of energy distribution.

## HOW BIG IS AN ATOM?

All matter, including your body, is made of atoms. Atoms are very tiny, though some are bigger than others. Just a grain of sand contains about 300,000,000,000,000,000,000 atoms— that's 300 hundred million trillion!

Later, galaxies form where there is most energy.

# THE UNIVERSE HAS A SPEED LIMIT

If you turn on a lamp, you can see the light instantly. Light moves very, very fast—it travels at 300,000 km (186,000 miles) per hour. The Sun is so far away that sunlight takes about eight minutes to get to Earth. That's not much time, but when you start to think about things that are farther away, the time becomes more important. The next nearest star is so distant that it takes 4 years and 10 weeks for its light to get to us.

## A light year is a measure of distance, not time

The distance light can travel in a year is called a light year. Astronomers use light years to measure large distances in space. A light year is nearly 9.5 trillion km (6 trillion miles). Nothing at all can travel faster than light—the speed of light is the universe's speed limit.

A car moving at 80 km/h (50 mph) would take 13.5 million years to cover a light year. It would take 214 years just to cover the eight light minutes to the Sun!

Alpha Centauri A, 4.4 light years from Earth

Neptune, average 4.2 light hours from Earth

Moon, 1.3 light seconds from Earth

## Space and time

The most distant star we can see without a telescope is 16,300 light years away. The light we see from it now left the star 16,300 years ago—so we're seeing it as it was in the distant past. If it had exploded 300 years ago, we wouldn't know until 16,000 years from now when the light from the explosion would reach us.

A very powerful telescope can see even farther back—it can see billions of years into the past and examine how stars and galaxies formed. This works both ways. An alien on a planet 70 million light years away looking at Earth with a powerful telescope would see Earth as it was in the time of the dinosaurs. With a powerful enough telescope, they would see not modern buildings, but a landscape roamed by *Tyrannosaurus rex* and *Triceratops*, with pterosaurs flying above.

Andromeda Galaxy, 2.5 million light years from Earth

# THE INFLATING UNIVERSE

During cosmic inflation, the universe grew faster than the speed of light. That might sound as though it's breaking the rule that nothing can move faster than light—but nothing was moving! New bits of universe (extra space–time) appeared in what was there already—just as new space appears on the surface of a balloon you are inflating. It happened so fast that places which were once right next to each other ended up so far apart that it would never again be possible for light to travel between them.

# MAKING A UNIVERSE IN 15 MINUTES

**The universe was still much less than a second old after its cosmic growth spurt. But it was ready for its next adventure—making matter.**

the water in a puddle

manufactured objects

planets

the gas in a balloon

plants

rocks

mammals

Matter is really just energy doing something special in a particular place. You can think of matter crystallizing out of the energy that filled the universe. The first matter was tiny particles called "quarks" that would later combine to make the middles of atoms—and the atoms would combine to make everything around us.

## Hot and cold

As the universe expanded, it got cooler. It is still expanding, and still getting cooler, and now it's really cold in outer space. When matter is hot, the particles move quickly, with a lot of energy. As the temperature drops, particles have less energy.

## First things first

As the universe cooled, quarks bumping into each other were going slowly enough to stick together. Groups of three quarks made particles called protons and neutrons. Everything we can see in the universe is made with the protons and neutrons formed in the first second of the universe.

Once the quarks had got together, they were stuck for all time—protons and neutrons never break apart, and no more can be made now.

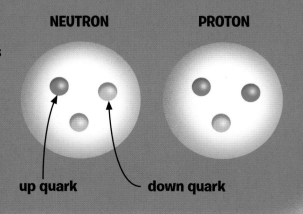
**NEUTRON**　　　**PROTON**

up quark　　　down quark

20

## Getting sticky

The protons and neutrons carried on whizzing around, and when they collided they, too, began to stick together. There were more protons than neutrons, so lots of protons were left over.

A proton is found in the middle (nucleus) of a hydrogen atom. Hydrogen is a gas, and it's the lightest chemical there is. When neutrons and protons first stuck together, they eventually formed groups of four—two protons and two neutrons. This is what makes the middle of a helium atom—helium is the gas that fills the floating balloons you sometimes get at parties. Later, all the other matter in the universe would be made by hydrogen and helium sticking together to build bigger atoms.

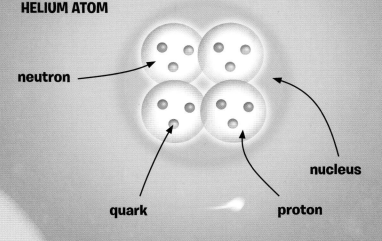

**HELIUM ATOM**

electron

neutron

nucleus

quark

proton

birds

# MATTER AND ANTI-MATTER

As well as all the matter around us, a lot of anti-matter also appeared in that first second— anti-protons, anti-neutrons, anti-electrons, and so on. Whenever a bit of anti-matter meets a corresponding bit of matter—an anti-proton and a proton, for instance—they instantly cancel each other out, becoming nothing. Luckily, there was slightly more matter than anti-matter—otherwise, everything would have been destroyed in the first second and we wouldn't be here!

Matter and anti-matter destroy each other instantly.

matter

anti-matter

As well as the protons and neutrons, there were also electrons and photons whizzing about during the universe's first second. These are tiny bits of energy, much smaller than protons and neutrons. Electrons carry electrical charge—the electricity that powers lights and computers. Photons are little parcels of electromagnetic radiation, such as light.

## Making atoms

Electrons have a negative electrical charge and protons have a positive charge, so they're attracted to each other. For hundreds of thousands of years, the protons and electrons were moving so fast that if they collided, they just bounced off each other. But as the universe carried on growing and cooling, they all slowed down a bit. After 379,000 years, it was cool enough for electrons and protons to stick together when they collided, making the first atoms. Single protons grabbed an electron and became hydrogen atoms. Helium nuclei grabbed two electrons (one for each proton), making helium atoms.

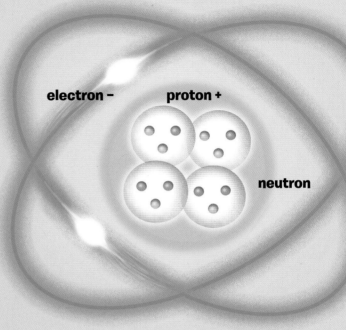

electron –    proton +

neutron

## MOSTLY SPACE

Most of an atom is empty space. The middle is very tiny, and the electrons are a very long way away from it. If the nucleus of a hydrogen atom was as big as a pea, the atom would be 350 m (1,150 ft) across—70,000 times the size of the pea. And if the nucleus was the Sun, the electron would be farther away than the planet Neptune.

## Orange is the new black

The light that flashed out at that moment was orange. Scientists can work this out by calculating the temperature of the universe at the time.

The universe isn't orange any more. Now if we look into space, it's black. The wavelength of the light released then has stretched as the universe has got colder. It's now stretched so much that it's mostly microwaves. We can't see microwaves, which is why space looks black.

**The first light to shine through the fog was orange.**

## Making space for light

As soon as the nuclei and electrons got together to make atoms, the universe became transparent. When it was clogged up with electrons, protons, and helium nuclei, photons didn't have enough room to move around quickly. They couldn't get far before bumping into something. The effect was like shining a flashlight into fog. Afterward, the photons had a clear path, and light flashed out for the first time.

When it's hot, particles move quickly.

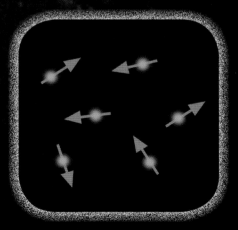

When it's colder, particles move more slowly and are less likely to collide.

# THE UNIVERSE TAKES A SELFIE

We can still trace the burst of energy from when the photons were set free. It serves as a map of how energy was distributed in the universe at the time. That distribution in energy grew from the slight differences that were fixed by cosmic inflation. It's as though the universe took a selfie 379,000 years after the Big Bang, and we can still see it!

## Cosmic microwaves

The burst of energy that happened 379,000 years after the Big Bang is called cosmic microwave background radiation (CMBR). This is because it is cosmic (meaning it is everywhere in the universe, or cosmos), it forms a background to all other radiation, and it is strongest in the microwave part of the spectrum.

## SEE FOR YOURSELF

You can hear the radiation from the Big Bang if you de-tune an old style (non-digital) radio. Part of the background hiss is made by the photons that were once the orange light, but their wavelength has changed over billions of years so that now they are radio waves.

## The lumpy universe

Scientists can make a map of the CMBR that shows the "lumpiness" of the universe. It's a snapshot of the radiation from anywhere that's exactly the right distance from Earth for the radiation burst to reach us right now. That distance is to the edge of the observable universe—as far as we will ever be able to see, no matter how good our telescopes become.

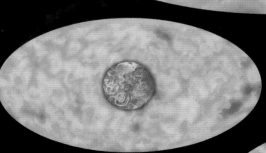

CNBR from Earth.

From a planet in another galaxy, the CMBR would look different.

24

## How big is the universe?
The observable universe is all of the universe that we can see and get information about. That doesn't mean it's all there is—the whole universe could be much bigger. The edge of the observable universe is 46.5 billion light years away in every direction, so the observable universe is 93 billion light years across.

### Light from far, far away
If the universe is 13.8 billion years old, it seems we should be able to see as far as 13.8 billion light years in every direction. But we can see farther than that. As the universe expands, more space appears between Earth and objects that are far away. Space has been added between us and a distant galaxy after its light started moving toward us. The starting point is moving away from us, so light has effectively "cheated" and jumped ahead.

# STARTING WITH STARS

**After the burst of light as photons began to move freely through the universe, the universe was dark again. For 180 million years, there was nothing to see, and no more light to see it by, in the "cosmic dark ages."**

At last, the darkness came to an end as the first stars began to shine. Something similar to the universe we now inhabit began to emerge from the blackness of space.

These first stars were huge and brilliant, burning hundreds or thousands of times as brightly as our Sun. They would not last long, but they made everything that followed possible, right up to our own existence.

# A SPONGY UNIVERSE

If you could have stood in the universe when it was 100 million years old,
you would have seen nothing—just emptiness spreading all around.
But although it was dark, it was not quite the same everywhere.

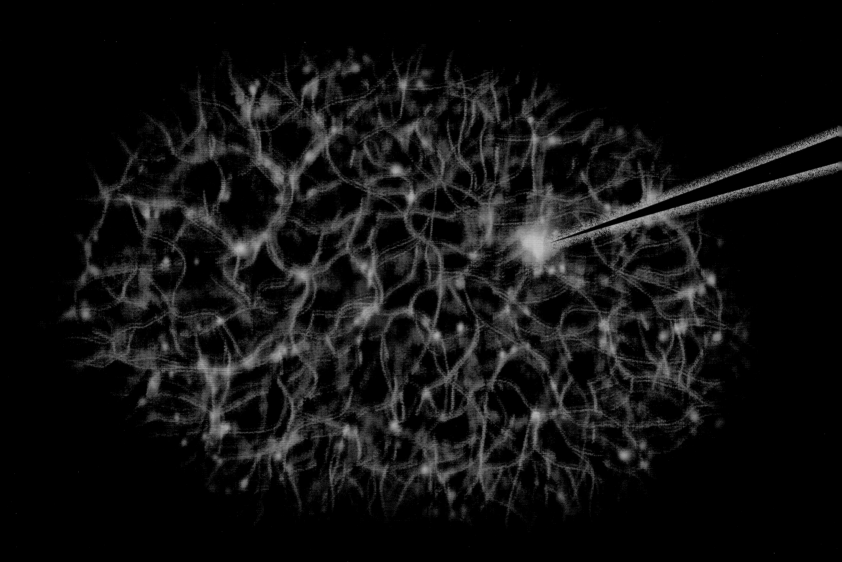

## Gases and gravity

The only matter in the universe was the atoms of the two first gases, hydrogen and helium. We are used to gases spreading out everywhere evenly. That's what they do in everyday life. If you open a packet of smelly food, the smell is instantly carried around the room in the air. But a room has only a small volume—a gas released in a much larger space acts a bit differently.

The gases of Earth's atmosphere are thickest near the ground where gravity is strongest, and they get thinner and thinner the higher we go. At the top of the atmosphere, they leak away into space. The whole atmosphere doesn't rush out into space, though, as gravity holds most of it close to the planet.

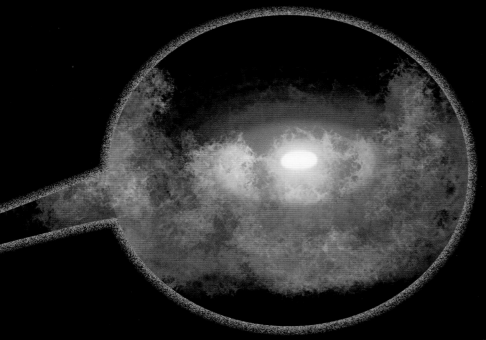

## Lumpy space

The early universe had patches where the gas was dense and patches where it was more spread out. This followed the pattern of the of the universe before cosmic inflation. In the places where gas was thickest, gravity was strongest—and gravity was strongest where the gas was thickest! It's a bit of a chicken-and-egg situation—clumps of gas produced gravity, and gravity attracted more gas.

## Hot spots

The universe's selfie, the pattern of the cosmic background radiation, shows the areas of hot and cold (or areas of more and less energy) that were frozen in place at the end of cosmic inflation. The difference in temperature was only tiny to start with, giving the universe just a slightly uneven texture.

Later, gas clustered in the "hot spots." Where there was most gas, gravity pulled the gas even closer together, forming clumps. Those clumps drew in more and more gas from nearby, making the gaps more gappy and the clumps more clumpy.

The result was a universe rather like a sponge, with strands or filaments that were streams of dense gas with gaps in between. If you could have moved through it, it would have been a bit warmer where the gas clumped together and colder in the vast, empty spaces. The universe still has this structure, but on a much larger scale. Later, stars and galaxies grew in the clumpy areas.

# THE BIRTH OF A STAR

**Incredibly, the giant spongy structure made just of gas clouds and empty space transformed over millions of years into stars burning brightly in the darkness.**

## From strings to nearly stars

The streaming filaments (long, slender bodies) of gas wound over and through each other, with the gas even more dense at the points where filaments crossed and combined. Clouds of gas became increasingly dense and lumpy until the densest areas collapsed in under their own gravity.

The collapse of a gas cloud became like a runaway train, going faster and faster. The pressure and temperature at the middle of the clumps increased until they reached a tipping point. The gas was so densely packed it became hot enough to glow. This was the first glimmering of what would later become true starlight.

The pockets of super-dense glowing gas were not yet stars, but protostars. They poured out light because they were so hot, in the way that a hot object on Earth glows—but they were not yet doing the work of a star.

The huge cloud of gas is called a molecular cloud. Stars still form in them today, and they can be hundreds of light years across.

## Around and about

A protostar is surrounded by more gas that moves toward it, but can't make it to the middle of the cloud. This gas forms a disk whirling around the protostar. The protostar, too, starts to turn. The dense, crossing points of the filaments of gas became vast, spinning clumps of gas, glowing with bright light and producing searing heat.

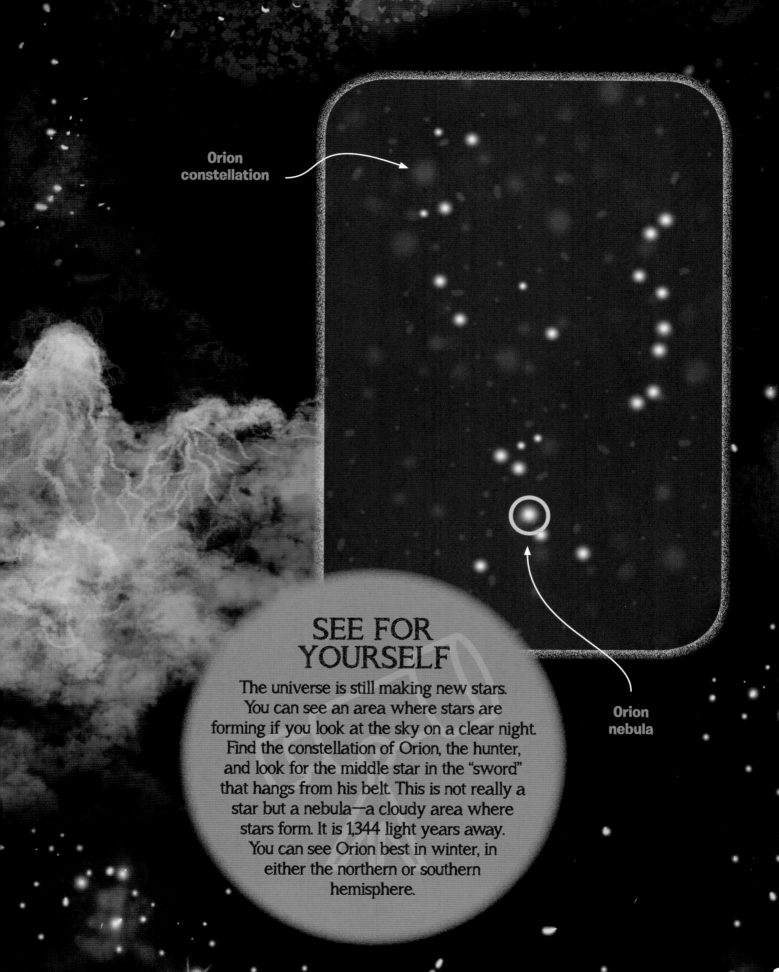

**Orion constellation**

**Orion nebula**

## SEE FOR YOURSELF

The universe is still making new stars. You can see an area where stars are forming if you look at the sky on a clear night. Find the constellation of Orion, the hunter, and look for the middle star in the "sword" that hangs from his belt. This is not really a star but a nebula—a cloudy area where stars form. It is 1,344 light years away. You can see Orion best in winter, in either the northern or southern hemisphere.

# SEEING WITH HEAT

You only need to stand in bright sunlight to notice that a star pours out energy. The light is dazzling and the heat can be intense. Light and heat are just parts of a whole spectrum of energy that our local star blasts out into space. All these types of energy are part of the electromagnetic spectrum (see page 15).

### Red + orange + yellow + green + ...
If you've ever seen a rainbow, you've seen how white light is made up of a whole range of shades that we traditionally divide into seven—red, orange, yellow, green, blue, indigo, and violet. There is no real boundary between these. Light is waves of energy, and how it looks depends on its wavelength. We see sunlight as white, but it's really a mix of light of lots of wavelengths. The objects around us look red, brown, purple or whatever because they reflect some of the light and absorb some of it. An object that reflects red light looks red.

## More than light
When you sit in the sunshine, you notice that sunlight is also warm. The heat pumped out by the Sun and other stars is energy with a different wavelength. In the spectrum, it's right next to visible light and is called infrared.

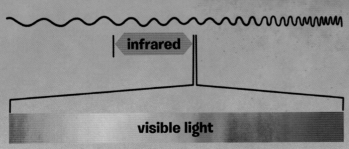

infrared

visible light

## Stars ramp up the heat

As protostars start to glow, they produce infrared before they produce visible light. Next they produce red light, and after that yellow and then white light—just as something heating in a fire feels warm before it starts to glow, then glows first red, then yellow, and finally white as it gets hotter and hotter. This means that when protostars first start to heat up, there's nothing to see—they aren't producing any visible light yet. Luckily, scientists can spot them using telescopes that can "see" infrared.

**Hot**

**Cold**

## Seeing in the dark

Infrared goggles and telescopes show things we can't see in visible light. They produce heat maps, with hotter areas being brighter and colder areas being dimmer. Using infrared telescopes, astronomers can see objects that are not yet glowing with visible light. They can also see more detail in objects that are glowing, because they can map areas that are hotter or colder.

## SEE FOR YOURSELF

If you have ever roasted marshmallows over a fire, you will have seen something that is so hot it glows. The burning wood or coal of a fire glows red-hot. When something is even hotter, it can glow yellow and even white.

# BURNING BRIGHT

When a proto-star becomes 0.08 (nearly a tenth) the mass of the Sun, it begins to "burn" the hydrogen that makes it up. It becomes a star at this point, and starts to glow much more brightly.

## A squash and a squeeze

The hydrogen atoms in the middle of a star are under immense pressure, squeezed unimaginably close together. They are so close together, that the middle of the Sun is eight times as dense as a lump of gold. A teaspoon of material from the Sun's core would weigh about 0.73 kg (1.6 lb) on Earth.

With much less space to move in, hydrogen atoms collide all the time—and when they do, it's a high-energy crash. They can't break, and they don't bounce apart because there isn't room. Instead, they stick together. This is called nuclear fusion, and it makes a new chemical element. Hydrogen atoms squashed together make helium—the other gas that was present in the early universe.

## Light squeezed out

It takes four hydrogen atoms to make one helium atom, but they don't all gang up at once. First, two hydrogen atoms collide, and then another joins them, making a group of three. When two groups of three collide, they make one helium atom and throw out two hydrogen atoms.

When hydrogen atoms stick together, they release photons—tiny parcels of energy. The photons stream from the Sun as light and heat—sunlight!

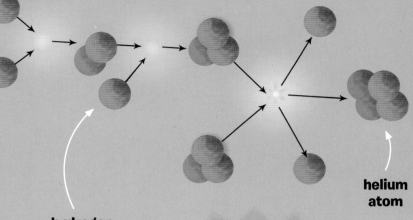

**hydrogen atom**

**helium atom**

## STAR PERSONALITY

# Celia Payne

Celia Payne worked out that stars are mostly hydrogen and helium in 1925. She was a British astronomer working in the USA. It seems incredible that vast stars can be made just of gas, and of the lightest gases in the universe. At the time, no one thought she could possibly be right—but she was.

## Really energetic

Although each atomic crash makes only a teeny, tiny bit of energy, there are so many collisions that it adds up to a massive amount. The Sun uses up between 600 and 700 million tonnes of hydrogen every single second. That's the weight of about 100 million large elephants. These collisions release 4,000 trillion times as much energy as all the power stations in the USA.

Don't worry that the Sun or other stars will be used up quickly. There is a very, very large number of atoms in our Sun, which means that a hydrogen atom will take an average of about 5 billion years to become part of a helium atom.

# HOW THE LIGHT GETS OUT

The middle of a star produces so much energy that the temperature is millions of degrees. The bigger the star, the higher the temperature, so the first, huge stars were incredibly hot in the middle.

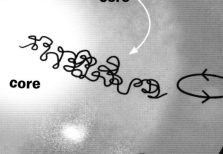

**photon's random path from core**

**core**

## Photons are not on a mission

Photons start off in the middle of a star, but they have to get out for us to see the star. The middle of the star is very dense and crowded, so the photon bumps into lots of other particles and keeps bouncing off in random directions. It's not even trying to get out—it's just bumbling around, moving in whatever direction its collisions take it.

Eventually, a photon gets to the edge of a star and can zoom off into space and reach our eyes or telescopes. Once it gets out, it travels at the speed of light—an incredibly fast 300,000 km per second (186,000 miles per second). Deep within the star, it can barely move.

In a star the size of the Sun, a photon takes on average 200,000 years to reach the surface from the middle, but it can take as much as 50 million years. It goes backward and forward, wandering around randomly until it just happens to get near enough to the surface to escape. It then takes just eight minutes to get from the Sun to Earth. A photon stuck in the core will move about 13 cm (5 inches) in eight minutes.

## Pushing and pulling

Photons escaping from the core of a star produce an outward pressure. On its own, that pressure would make the star grow larger. Gravity provides an inward pressure, pulling all parts of the star toward the middle, working to make the star smaller. When the pressures produce by gravity and by hydrogen burning in the core are equal, the star stays the same size. Astronomers call this a main sequence star.

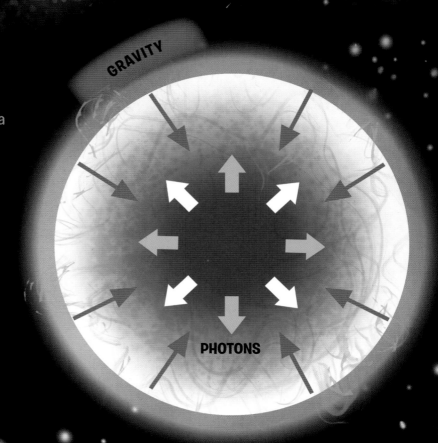

GRAVITY

PHOTONS

## STAR OR SOIL?

Each bucketful of the Sun's core produces only about as much heat as the same volume of a compost heap. That's because each collision of hydrogen atoms only makes a tiny amount of energy. The Sun is so big, though, that all together this adds up to a massive amount of energy.

# LIVE FAST, DIE YOUNG

The first stars were huge, possibly up to 1,000 times the mass of the Sun. They used up their hydrogen quickly, surviving only for a few million years. A star the size of our Sun will keep going for around 11 billion years—more than a thousand times as long.

## Shifting shades

When you look up at the night sky, all the stars you can see look white. In reality, stars can shine with blue, white, yellow, orange, red, and even green light depending on their temperature. The first stars were blue, and shone tens of thousands of times as brightly as the Sun. They were scorching hot, with a surface far hotter than the Sun's.

Astronomers use the Harvard system to group stars by their temperature, which they work out from the type of light the stars put out. Stars that emit mostly blue light are the hottest, at up to 53,000°C (95,500°F). The coolest are a dull red, and are only about 2,000°C (3,600°F) at their surface. The scale is ordered from the hottest to the coolest stars, using the letters: OBAFGKM.

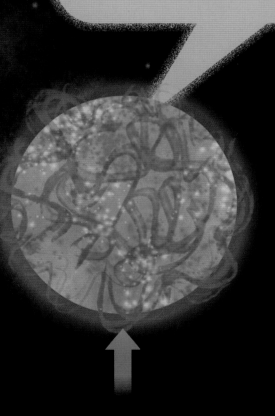

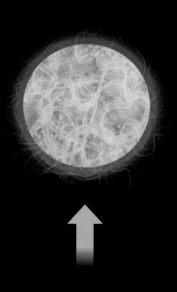

**O**
Up to 53,000°C (95,500°F) and 15 times the width of the Sun; lives only 2–10 million years

**B**
Average temperature 20,000°C (36,000°F); lives 10–150 million years

**A**
Average temperature 8,300°C (15,000°F); lives 300 million to 1 billion years

# WHY ARE THERE NO GREEN STARS?

**visible light**

Because of the way our eyes work, we will always see greenish stars as white—but our scientific tools can tell us that some stars put out more green light than yellow or blue light. The Sun is one of them—it produces light across the spectrum, which mixes together and looks white, but it's actually a bit greener than it is red, yellow, or blue.

## Burned out

Today, most stars in the universe are fairly small and cool. More than 90 percent of all stars are yellow, orange, or red (G, K, or M). Fewer than one in a million is a large blue star, but in the early universe most stars were giant blue stars.

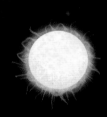

**G**
Average temperature 5,500°C (10,000°F); lives 8–12 billion years. Our Sun is a G-class star

**M**
Average temperature 2,900°C (5,200°F); lives 68–700 billion years

**F**
Average temperature 6,200°C (11,200°F); lives 2–3 billion years

**K**
Average temperature 4,200°C (7,600°F); lives 22–45 billion years

# BACK TO BLACK

**When the first gigantic stars ran out of hydrogen, they came to a catastrophic end, becoming black holes—areas of space from which nothing, not even light, escapes.**

## Turning out the lights

Stars can die in many ways (see next chapter), but the very first large stars might have turned almost instantly into black holes. "Black hole" is not really a very good name, as a black hole is far from empty. It's crammed with matter, and is the densest thing there is. Imagine taking a star and squeezing it so hard that all the empty space is crushed out of it, even the space between and within atoms. Even the atoms are crushed out of existence.

A very massive early star might turn into a black hole with little warning. The core might get so hot that the photons become unstable and destroy each other. Then they wouldn't be moving outward, and there would be no pressure to balance out the gravity pulling the star inward. Gravity would pull all of the star to the middle, where it doesn't fit. There would be just a super-dense blob of matter that can go nowhere and sends out no light. To an outside observer, the star would simply turn off. All the matter is still there, but we can't see it. That's a black hole.

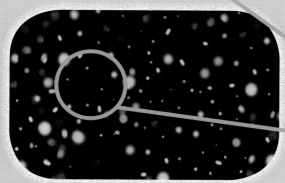

**The star has gone, leaving a black hole.**

## Holes in the universe

We can't see a black hole as it's tiny and completely black—but astronomers can tell where they are because they disrupt space around them. A black hole's gravity pulls in matter and energy from around it. If anything gets too close, it's dragged in and destroyed. If you don't want to be pulled into a black hole, the border not to cross is called the event horizon. Over the event horizon, nothing can escape, not even light. The whole area within the event horizon is dark.

# QUASARS: THE LIGHT AROUND A BLACK HOLE

Black holes pull on matter around them, which then whirls around. This spinning disk of gas and dust gets hotter and hotter as particles crash or rub together and glow. The disk is outside the event horizon, so we can see it—its light can escape. Some matter pulled toward the black hole just misses and bounces back out as a super-fast jet of energy and particles. We can see that, too. This type of super-massive black hole and its radiation is called a quasar.

# A GALAXY OF STARS

Galaxies are vast collections of stars. Our Sun is part of a galaxy called the Milky Way, which contains 100–400 billion stars. There are probably between 200 billion and two trillion galaxies in the observable universe.

The Milky Way

## Seeing stars

Every star you can see in the night sky is in the Milky Way, and there are many, many more that you can't see. Whichever galaxy a living being is in, the only stars it will be able to see are in its own galaxy. Galaxies are so large and widely spaced that it's impossible to see individual stars in another galaxy.

## Which came first?

No one is quite sure how or when the first galaxies came about. Stars might have formed in groups right from the start, or they might have each started separately and then come together into galaxies.

## A hole in the middle

All large galaxies probably have a super-massive black hole in the middle. The black hole can have billions of times the mass of the Sun, but be smaller than the solar system. Stars orbit the central black hole, but they are too far away to be pulled into it. Galaxies possibly first grew around the black holes made by the first stars dying.

## Smashing times

Galaxies move through space all the time, and sometimes they collide. This sounds like a major catastrophe, but as galaxies are mostly empty space, few stars will actually crash into each other. The galaxies generally merge quite peacefully. Large galaxies might have grown from small galaxies merging.

Our own galaxy is on a collision course with the Andromeda galaxy, with both moving at 402,000 km (250,000 miles) per hour. They will meet in about four billion years and merge.

### Galaxies get together

Galaxies are unimaginably huge, but they don't live alone. They form groups, or clusters, and even superclusters. Our galaxy is part of a supercluster of 100,000 galaxies. Clusters are separated by vast empty spaces. This is the sponge-like texture of the baby universe, but now with filaments made of groups of galaxies that are millions of light years long.

## SEE FOR YOURSELF

On a clear dark night, you might be able to see another galaxy, outside the Milky Way. The Andromeda galaxy looks like a small fuzzy patch of light between the constellations Andromeda and Cassiopeia.

Cassiopeia constellation

Andromeda galaxy

43

# DEATH AND REBIRTH OF STARS

The stars in all their forms have made our universe what it is. The stars we see today are the same in some ways as the early stars, yet they are very different in other ways. They still forge hydrogen into helium at their core, releasing huge amounts of energy to flood space with light and heat. But their lives follow different patterns, and they end in different ways. Many will last billions of years rather than just millions of years. Some stars that are shining now might even last trillions of years—far longer than the entire history of the universe so far. Some will still end as black holes, but many more will have a very different fate.

# THE END IS NIGH

A star fuses hydrogen at its core for millions or billions of years, but eventually it starts to run out. There are too few hydrogen atoms left to collide with each other easily. The star begins the next phase of its life, but it can't go on for much longer—and it's not going to end well!

## Pushing and pulling

The star's gravity still pulls it inward, squashing everything in the middle even closer together. Normally, the inward pressure is balanced by pressure pushing outward from the inside. When there is not enough hydrogen left to fuse, that pressure stops and gravity wins. It pulls the star inward more and more vigorously until the pressure in the core is so great that the helium atoms fuse together.

The core of the star then has two layers—one in the very middle fusing helium, and a shell outside it with the leftover hydrogen. The outer shell is cooler, but much larger as it's blown away from the middle of the star. If you were on a planet near the star, you would be in trouble.

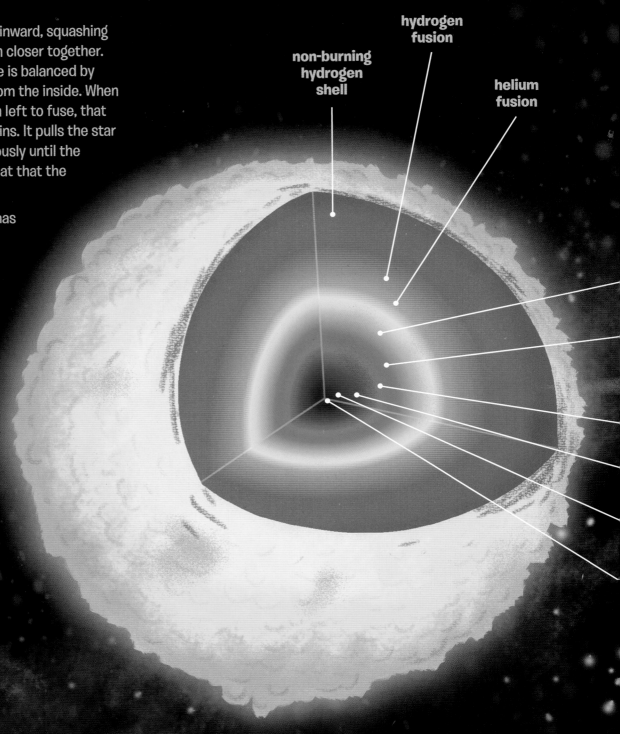

non-burning
hydrogen
shell

hydrogen
fusion

helium
fusion

carbon fusion

oxygen fusion

neon fusion

magnesium fusion

silicon fusion

iron core

## A slippery slope

The star has made the helium by fusing four hydrogen atoms, so there can never be as many helium atoms as there were hydrogen atoms. The core gets through the helium much more quickly than it got through the hydrogen. It fuses helium to make carbon, taking three helium atoms to make one carbon atom. When it's fused most of the helium, the same thing happens again—the star collapses a bit, blows its leftover helium out of the way, and gets to work on the carbon it's made.

This keeps going, with the star growing ever larger until it is left with a core of solid iron. Iron is the heaviest atom a star can make, so then it's stuck. These hugely inflated stars are called red giants—they are cool, so look red rather than white, and they are giant!

## The end of the road

What happens next depends on the size of the star. The largest stars end their lives in a catastrophic explosion, but smaller ones shrink to a tiny, hot core.

# WHEN STARS EXPLODE

The largest red giants—supergiants—end their lives in a catastrophic explosion called a "supernova." A supernova is one of the most spectacular events in the universe. It makes a dramatic display that lasts hundreds or thousands of years.

## Big enough to bang

A star 10–20 times the mass of our Sun can die in a blaze of glory. After burning for 10–20 million years, it grows to a red giant with an iron core the size of Earth. When fusion stops completely, gravity pulls everything inward almost instantly. The core shrinks at up to 70,000 km/second (43,500 miles per second), and the star collapses. But the middle is already full, so it all bounces back out immediately. The shockwaves blast the star apart. In just a few seconds, the star throws out more energy than our Sun will produce in its entire lifetime.

## A quick death

A star might take 10 billion years to fuse all its hydrogen, but it will spend only 600 years fusing carbon. It will run out of oxygen after six months, and can manage only one day fusing silicon into iron before its end comes.

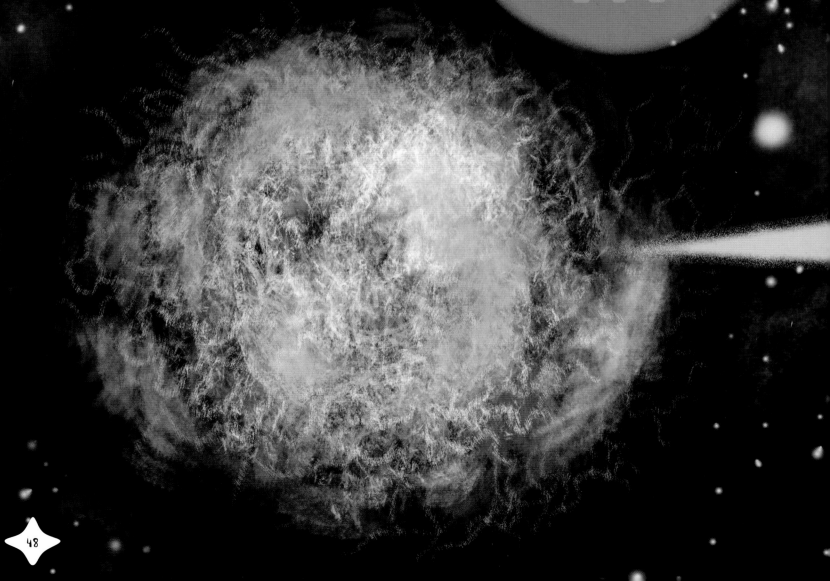

48

## Star bright

A supernova can glow more brightly than anything else in the sky. Supernovas close enough to see without a telescope are rare—the last was in 1604. It was 20,000 light years from Earth, but shone so brightly it was visible by day for three weeks, and at night for 18 months. In 400 years, the cloud of dust and gas from the supernova has grown to be 14 light years across.

Somewhere in our galaxy, a star goes supernova every 50 years, and somewhere in the known universe, a star goes supernova about every second.

## Made in the death throes of stars

The heaviest metals are not made in normal stars, but are forged in supernovas when the immense pressure of the explosion forces large atoms together and fuses them.

**Uranium**, and other radioactive elements such as plutonium, are used to power nuclear power stations.

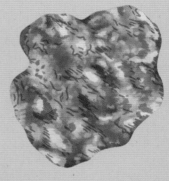

**Silver** is the best conductor of heat and electricity.

**Mercury** is the only metal that is liquid at room temperature.

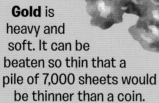

**Gold** is heavy and soft. It can be beaten so thin that a pile of 7,000 sheets would be thinner than a coin.

**Bismuth** is a soft metal with a shiny, reflective surface. It's brittle and breaks easily.

# DYING EMBERS

**While the dramatic supernova leaves a giant remnant, the dead star in the middle is tiny. Astronomers can spot a supernova remnant easily—it's typically light years across. But the burned out core is the size of a city at most.**

## Atomic accident

When the core collapses catastrophically, the atoms in it are crushed until they are destroyed. The electrons are forced into the middle of the atoms so that they combine with the protons, turning into neutrons. As most of the space occupied by an atom is empty, and lies between the middle and the electrons, this makes the atoms much smaller. It also means they are turned entirely into a core of neutrons.

The lump of neutron matter is called a "neutron star." It's made just of neutrons with no empty space, and is the densest matter in the universe apart from a black hole. A neutron star can be two or three times the mass of the Sun, but is only the size of Manhattan. A piece of neutron star as small as a sugar cube contains as much mass as Mount Everest.

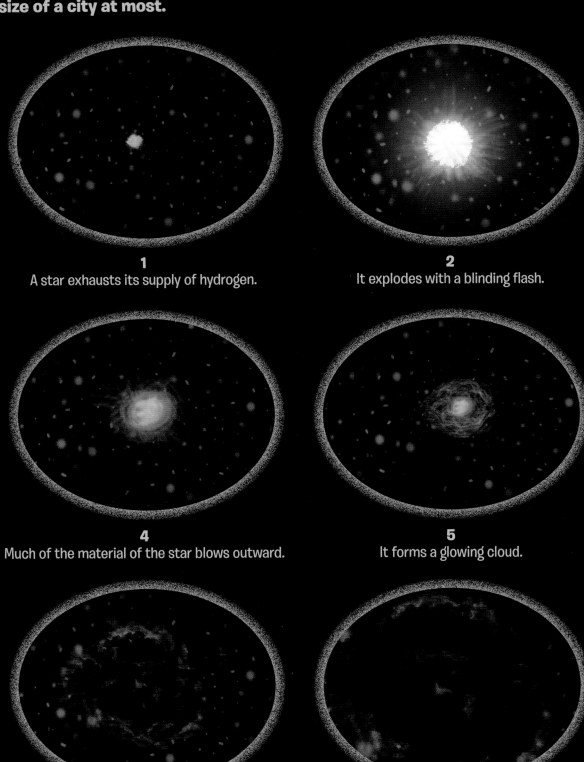

**1**
A star exhausts its supply of hydrogen.

**2**
It explodes with a blinding flash.

**4**
Much of the material of the star blows outward.

**5**
It forms a glowing cloud.

**7**
After 10,000 years, the remnant is
100 light years across.

**8**
The elements forged in the star are
scattered through space.

## Now you see them, now you don't

When stars 10–29 times the mass of the Sun go supernova, they leave a neutron star behind. Even larger stars leave a core so dense it is a black hole. Both black holes and neutron stars are tiny, dark, and hard to spot. Astronomers might see the supernova cloud around the core, but they can't easily see what it is in the middle.

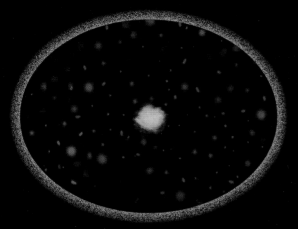

**3**
The glowing middle begins to grow.

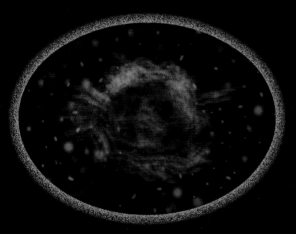

**6**
The supernova remnant expands into space.

**9**
In the middle, a tiny neutron star is all that remains

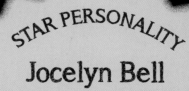

### Spinning stars

Neutron stars spin, rotating several times a second. They can suck in matter from other stars and then they go even faster. The fastest known neutron stars spin at a quarter of the speed of light. These super-fast neutron stars are pulsars. They beam out regular pulses of radiation as they spin, which is how we can tell they are there.

## STAR PERSONALITY

### Jocelyn Bell

British graduate student Jocelyn Bell found the first pulsar in 1967. When she found a radio signal that repeated every 1.3 seconds, astronomers wondered if it could be a signal from aliens. They worked out the true nature of pulsars when they found one in the middle of the Crab Nebula, left by a supernova in 1054.

# STARTING OVER

The explosion of a supernova hurls lots of new matter into space. It scatters the elements the star made during its lifetime, and also the new elements forged in the heat of the explosion. These can be used to make new stars—and eventually planets, too.

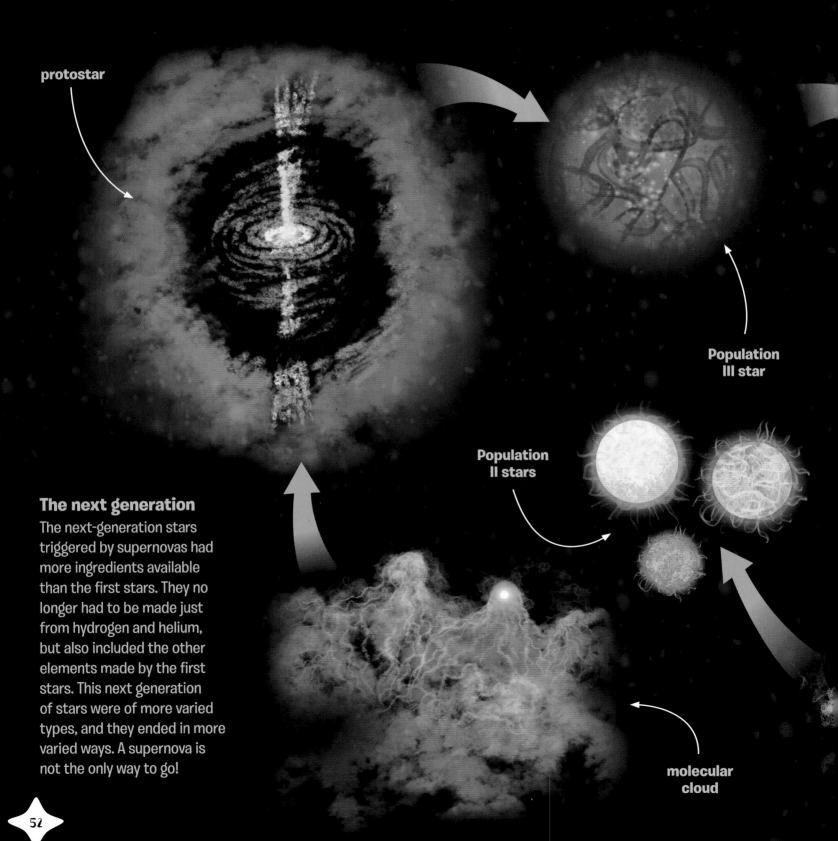

protostar

Population III star

Population II stars

molecular cloud

## The next generation

The next-generation stars triggered by supernovas had more ingredients available than the first stars. They no longer had to be made just from hydrogen and helium, but also included the other elements made by the first stars. This next generation of stars were of more varied types, and they ended in more varied ways. A supernova is not the only way to go!

## A bit of a shock

The shockwaves produced by a supernova rip through space. They can disrupt and squash molecular clouds nearby, triggering the creation of new stars.

**supernova**

**supernova remnants**

**material from the supernova, which enriches space**

## Populating space

Astronomers divide stars into Population I, Population II, and Population III stars. The oldest are Population III stars. They started with only hydrogen and a little helium, as this was all that there was in the universe when they formed. Population II stars came after the first generation of stars had lived and died and spread their materials around into space. They used the materials created in stars and supernovas, as well as still having a great deal of hydrogen and helium. Population I stars are the current generation of stars, including our Sun. They have all the naturally occurring elements and have more of them than Population II stars. They have material produced in all the stars that have existed before them.

As time goes by, more and more of the universe's original hydrogen and helium is forged into different elements. But don't worry—there is lots of unused hydrogen left, and the universe is not going to run out, even in billions more years.

### HOW DO WE KNOW?

Astronomers can work out the elements that are in a star by looking at the light that comes from it. Elements take in, and also shine out, light of specific wavelengths, so it's possible to work out what is there by looking at the light.

# GIANTS AND DWARFS

The early Population III stars were very large and burned through their hydrogen quickly. Most of the stars that have formed since are much smaller and last much longer. They are too small to make red supergiants and supernovas.

## From red to white

Stars the size of our Sun swell to red giants toward the end of their life. They don't have enough mass to collapse catastrophically. Instead, they blow out their outer layers with the elements they have made. This makes a ball of glowing gas around the star called a "planetary nebula." The name is a bit misleading—it has nothing to do with planets! The nebula is carried off into space, and its material will be used in future stars.

Just the dense core is left in the middle. Gravity has pulled the atoms so close together that they are squeezed and distorted, but not squashed into only neutrons. The core stops shrinking when the electrons in it are as close together as they can get. It is 200,000 times as dense as Earth. The core still glows white hot, and is called a white dwarf.

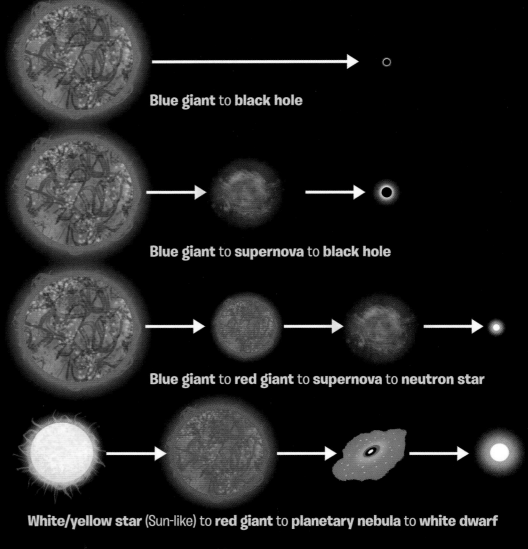

**Blue giant** to **black hole**

**Blue giant** to **supernova** to **black hole**

**Blue giant** to **red giant** to **supernova** to **neutron star**

**White/yellow star** (Sun-like) to **red giant** to **planetary nebula** to **white dwarf**

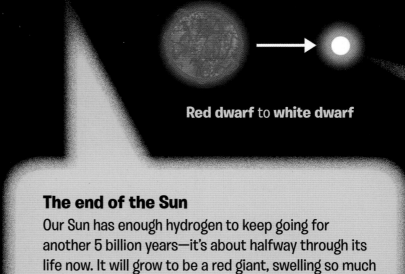

**Red dwarf** to **white dwarf**

## The end of the Sun
Our Sun has enough hydrogen to keep going for another 5 billion years—it's about halfway through its life now. It will grow to be a red giant, swelling so much its outer layers will reach as far as Earth's orbit.

## On and on

A white dwarf isn't working any more and can't stay hot and glowing forever. As it cools, its grow duller and darker.

Over trillions of years or more, a white dwarf will eventually fade to a dull, cold, black dwarf that produces no light. The universe is not old enough to have any black dwarfs yet.

white dwarf

## TOO SMALL TO BE OLD

Stars even smaller and cooler than the Sun are red dwarfs. They fuse their hydrogen slowly, and carry on working for trillions of years. The universe is too young to have any old or dying red dwarfs yet.

the star cools down

## Life on a white dwarf

You couldn't live on a white dwarf, but if you could go to one it would be a freaky experience. The solid crust is about 50 km (30 miles) thick, but the atmosphere is only a few cm (or inches) thick. If you dropped anything, it would fall extremely fast and shatter, spreading out over the surface on impact. The surface is perfectly smooth because gravity is strong enough to even it out completely.

black dwarf

# DARKER AND DARKER

The universe becomes more mysterious the more we find out about it. Astronomers now know just how much they don't know!

## In the dark

If the galaxies contained only the mass we can see (such as stars), they would rip apart as they spin so fast. To hold them together, they need more mass to make enough gravity. They need a lot more mass—about six times as much as they have.

That's a lot that is apparently missing, so it must mean we can only see a small portion of the matter in the universe. Astronomers call the missing mass "dark matter." It's probably not ordinary matter, such as dark stars or hidden planets, but a completely new type of matter.

## The ballooning universe

You might think it's bad enough that we can only see a little bit of the matter in the universe, but it turns out that things are even worse than that. In the 1990s, astronomers discovered that distant galaxies are moving away from each other faster than ever. Everyone had assumed that gravity would slow down the expansion of the universe, so this was a real surprise.

Until about 5 billion years ago, the universe grew steadily larger and larger. But since then, it's been expanding more quickly.

## Vera Rubin

Astronomer Vera Rubin worked out that dark matter must exist by calculating the speeds at which stars go around the middle of our galaxy. Their speeds show there is a lot more mass in the galaxy than we can see. A halo (ring) of dark matter around the galaxy would explain their speed.

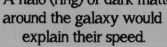

### There's a lot of nothing

As the universe expands, more empty space appears between galaxies and pushes them apart. That means more "nothing" is added to the universe! The force pushing galaxies apart has been called "dark energy" and it's the opposite of gravity. Gravity pulls objects together, but dark energy pushes them apart. No one understands how dark energy works or where it comes from.

Dark energy makes up even more of the universe than dark matter. For the universe to behave as it does, it must be made of 68 percent dark energy, 27 percent dark matter—and just 5 percent normal matter. "Normal" matter isn't normal at all, as it's by far the smallest part of the universe. Yet that part includes all the stars, planets, moons, and everything else we can see or measure.

# MAKING MORE MATTER

The stars poured out their newly made elements into space, but most things around us are not made of elements. They are made of more complicated chemicals called "compounds" that combine two or more elements.

## Elemental

There are 94 elements that occur naturally. These are all that are needed to build stars, planets, moons, comets, and all the other normal matter in the universe. Every element has a different design of atom, with a different number of protons in the nucleus. But to make the stuff around us—water, rock, plants, people, and everything else—the elements need to combine to make compounds.

separate atoms

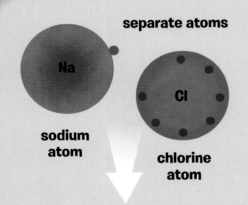

sodium
atom

chlorine
atom

## Atoms and molecules

When two or more atoms get together, they make a molecule. Molecules can be broken apart again to get the atoms back and make other molecules, though it's not always very easy to break them apart.

Which atoms will get together depends on how many electrons each has. Some atoms would be more stable if they had extra electrons and some would be better off with fewer. Atoms make molecules if they can share, give away, or gain electrons.

Here, an electron has been shared to make a molecule.

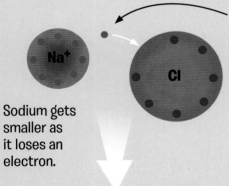

Sodium gets smaller as it loses an electron.

These molecules join together to make a crystal lattice compound.

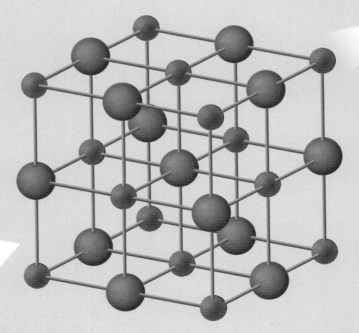

sodium chloride molecule (NaCl)

58

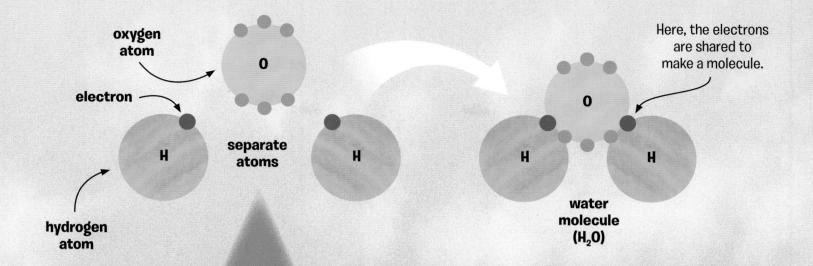

oxygen atom

electron

O

separate atoms

H

H

hydrogen atom

Here, the electrons are shared to make a molecule.

O

H

H

water molecule (H$_2$O)

## Water for worlds

Water is a compound made of hydrogen and oxygen, two gases. Each water molecule has one oxygen atom and two hydrogen atoms. The first water formed in gas clouds a billion years after the Big Bang. It was possible for water to form after the first stars had released oxygen into space, but not before. The oxygen combined with hydrogen to make pockets of water that first existed as a gas and later as tiny specks of ice.

The molecules needed to make rocks and even life-forms also started off in space. When the material to make planets clumped together in space, a lot of it was already in compounds that could build into rocks.

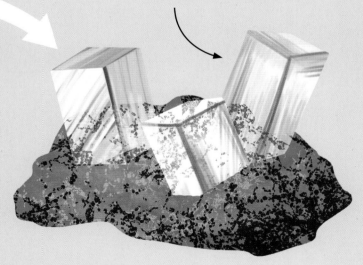

sodium chloride (salt) crystal on rock

## LIFE FROM SPACE?

Living things are made from lots of very complicated carbon compounds—large molecules with carbon, hydrogen and other atoms stuck together. Some of these carbon-based molecules are found in space. Scientists have found some of them on meteors. They are just the building blocks for life, but it's a good start! It could mean there is life in lots of places.

# WORLDS OF DUST AND GAS

After the first generation of stars had poured the elements they made into space, there was more raw material for making new stars. These new stars still fused hydrogen to produce energy. They didn't use the extra matter, but the extra matter was useful—it meant these stars could build planets. And not just planets, but moons, asteroids and comets, making whole systems of bodies in space, from massive balls of gas to solid lumps of metal.

Most of what we know about planets and moons comes from studying our own solar system, but stars elsewhere in the galaxy—and probably in other galaxies—also have planets. It's likely that some will be like the planets of our solar system, though many are very different.

# BUMPS AND LUMPS

**As a star forms at the middle of a collapsing cloud of dust and gas, the material that hasn't been pulled into it flattens into a disk whirling around it.**

## Bumps and bangs

In the disk, fast-moving particles of dust and gas collide and crash. Some stick when they bump into each other, making slightly bigger lumps. As the lumps and clumps get larger, their gravity attracts even more matter. The disk is filled with chunks flying around and crashing into each other. The bigger they grow, the more violent their collisions become. Some lumps stick together, some smash each other apart, and some just bounce off each other. Those that smash apart are soon absorbed in new collisions.

## Growing and growing

The larger a lump grows, the "stickier" it gets, as it has more gravity to pull in and hold onto more material. When the surviving lumps get to about 1 km (0.6 mile) across, they begin a runaway growth phase. They hurtle around the central star, gathering up more and more matter until they become mini planets, called "protoplanets" or "planetesimals." It takes less than a million years to grow planetesimals from dust grains.

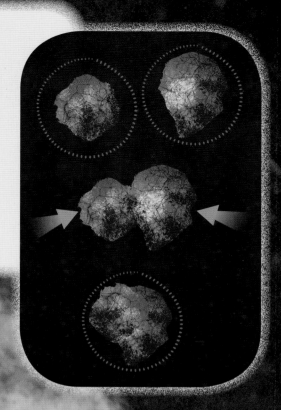

## HOW DO WE KNOW?

We know what's in space dust because some of it regularly falls to Earth as "micrometeorites," and some has been collected by space missions. This is just dust from our solar system, but dust around other stars is probably much the same.

## Dust, but no dust bunnies

The "dust" in the protoplanetary disk is not like the dust under your bed. That's mostly skin, hair, and bits of fabric from clothes and furnishings. The dust in space is a mix of elements, such as silicon and carbon, and compounds that have formed from two or more elements getting together. Some of these can be the type of carbon compounds that are needed to build living things. Others are forms of rock, like silicon oxide. The dust grains can be as small as a few molecules clinging together, or as large as 0.1 mm (1/250th of an inch)—which is not very large at all!

Most of the cloud is gas, not dust. It's so cold that some gases are frozen and form grains of solid ice. Oxygen is a gas on Earth, but exists as ice grains in space.

# PLANET BUILDING

Eventually, some of the lumps grow large enough to be small planets. An object that has grown large enough to clear a space for its orbit around the Sun is in the running to be counted as a planet. It has enough gravity to clear its orbit of all smaller bits and pieces, which it has dragged into itself.

## Planets in the round

The lumps of nearly planet spin on their axes, just as Earth spins once every 24 hours. If the lump is large enough—at least 1,000 km (600 miles) across—its gravity will tug on all parts of the surface until it pulls the planet into a ball. On a ball, each bit of the surface is the same distance from the middle as every other bit. A lump that has cleared its orbit and become spherical under its own gravity has made it as a planet!

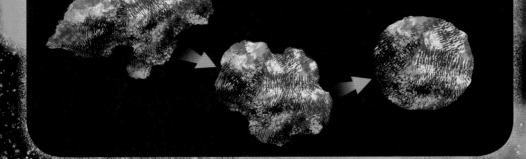

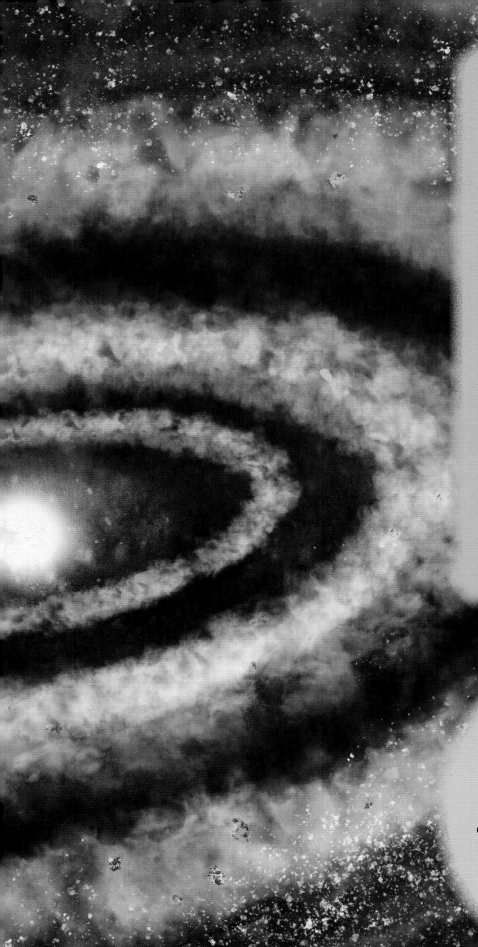

## Rocky planets and gassy planets

In our solar system, there are rocky planets near the Sun, and gas and ice planets farther away from it. The rocky planets are Mercury, Venus, Earth, and Mars. Then there's a gap and a group of gas and ice planets: Jupiter, Saturn, Uranus, and Neptune. Rocky planets form nearer to the Sun because the materials they are made of—largely rock and metal—have the lowest boiling and melting points. These materials are solid even close to the Sun. Material needs to be solid to form clumps and to have a chance of growing into a planet.

Gas and ice planets form farther from the Sun as their matter only freezes and becomes solid at very low temperatures. A gas giant grows around a rocky core from little frozen lumps of gas collecting around it and sticking together. Gas and ice planets form beyond a "frost line" or "snowline." This is where it's far enough from the Sun for chemicals that are liquid or gas on Earth to freeze.

## BIG PLANETS BULGE IN THE MIDDLE

Large planets have a bulgy middle, while smaller planets are more spherical. A spot on the equator (middle) of a spinning planet has to move faster to complete a full circle than a spot at either pole (end). The bits at the equator are always on the verge of being hurled into space. Gravity manages to hold onto them—but only just.

# ROCKY PLANETS

As a rocky planet grows larger, it separates into layers. The heaviest types of material end up in the middle and the lightest parts at the surface. On Earth, an atmosphere of light gases is wrapped around a solid surface of rock and a central core of metal.

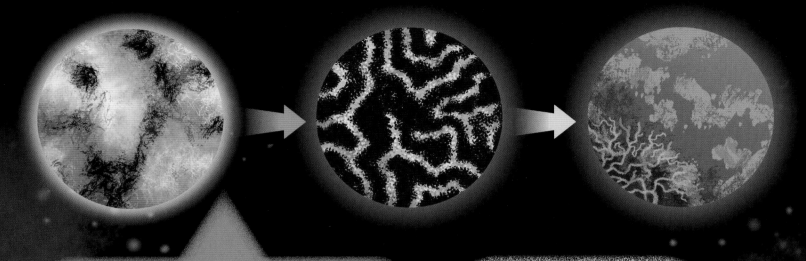

### A bit of a mix up

The material that collects together to make up a rocky planet includes different types of rock and metal. Some of the chunks also have lighter materials sticking to them or already trapped inside, such as water and gases. As these come together, all the materials are mixed up.

The pressure of all the material pushing toward the middle heats up the baby planet, especially in the middle. It is so hot that even rock and metal can melt. While the planet is mostly molten, the heavy metals in it are pulled toward the middle more strongly than the lighter rock, water, and gases. Over a long time, all the metal sinks to the middle, forming a heavy metal core. A thick layer of hot, molten rock forms around it. This would have happened to all the rocky planets in the solar system, and probably in other star systems, too.

### Rocky neighbours
Our solar system has four inner, rocky planets.

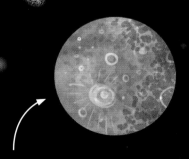

**Mercury** is closest to the Sun. It has a large metal core and a surface of bare rock. It's very cold at night and very hot by day.

## Hot and bothered

For millions of years, other lumps of rock and ice, big and small, continue to hurtle through space, bombarding the newly forming planets. Although the molten surface cools and hardens, each new impact breaks and melts it again. Smaller impacts melt an area, but large impacts can re-melt the whole surface.

## HOW DO WE KNOW?

The Moon, Mars, and Mercury all have craters that are the scars of asteroids and meteors crashing into the surface long ago. The same would have happened on Earth, but Earth's surface is weathered by wind and water, so the craters have largely worn away.

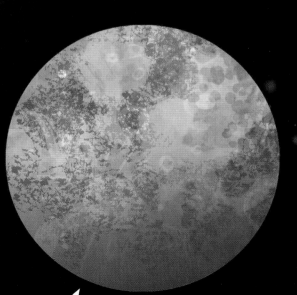

Venus is the hottest rocky planet. It has a thick atmosphere of carbon dioxide that keeps heat locked in.

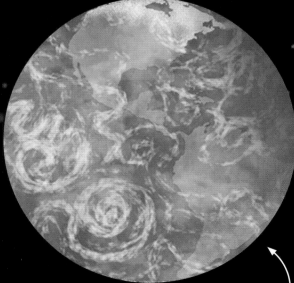

Earth is the only planet with oceans of liquid water on the surface, and the only one known to host life.

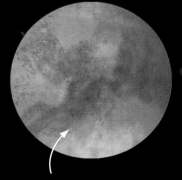

Mars is colder than Earth and has ice on the surface. In the past it had running water—we can see the marks it has left in the surface.

# AIR AND WATER

Rocky planets are not entirely made of rock. They can have water or another liquid on the surface or underground. They can also have snow or ice (frozen liquids). And they can have an atmosphere—a cloak of gases.

## First air

At first, planets capture hydrogen and helium from the protoplanetary disk as they form. This doesn't last long, though. These gases are very light. They are mostly hydrogen and helium, the same gases that make up the star. Because they are light, it's hard for the planet's gravity to hold onto them and they can easily escape into space. When the star becomes active, solar wind pouring from it whisks the light gases away.

## Excuse me!
## Planetary burps

A planet can get a new atmosphere of gases escaping from inside by a process called "outgassing." Gas bubbles up through hot molten rock, or comes out of volcanoes. These gases were mixed in with the chunks that went to build the planet. Earth and Venus both have a thick atmosphere made in this way.

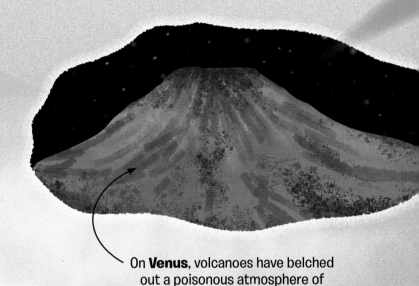

On **Venus**, volcanoes have belched out a poisonous atmosphere of carbon dioxide and sulfuric acid

On **Earth**, volcanoes bring up gas and water from within the planet.

## Weather forecast

A planet with an atmosphere can have weather—and the weather on Venus is very, very bad! Winds whip around the planet at super-storm force, and the clouds are made of burning acid. Winds travel at up to 360 kph (220 mph), which is 60 times as fast as the planet itself rotates. On Earth, winds go at only about a tenth or a fifth of Earth's own speed.

On **Earth**, we have water as liquid, as solid (ice) and as gas. We can't see water as a gas, but we can see it when it condenses to make clouds.

## A swim or a snowball fight?

The rocky chunks that form a planet also carry water into the mix. Water rises to the surface and escapes, coming out of volcanoes as a gas. Then it can condense (turn to liquid) and fall to the surface as water (rain) or ice (snow).

Earth has liquid water and also vast sheets of ice at the poles and high on mountains. The Moon and Mars have water only as ice. Without an atmosphere to keep them warm, these places are too cold for ice to melt. Rocky planets can have water frozen underground or in underground lakes or seas, too.

Korolev crater on **Mars** has probably been filled with ice for millions of years.

# GAS AND ICE PLANETS

**Not all planets have a solid surface you can stand on. Gas and ice planets are great balls of gas and slushy ice, held in shape by their gravity, and with only a tiny solid core right in the middle.**

## Chilly neighbours

Our solar system has a group of giant gas and ice planets whirling through space, beyond the rocky planets. They are Jupiter, Saturn, Uranus, and Neptune.

**Saturn**

**GAS GIANTS**

**Jupiter**

## Making gas and ice planets

Far from a star, liquids, and even gases freeze into ice grains. The middle of a gas planet forms in the same way as a rocky planet, with grains of rock and ice combining to make the core. A thick layer of gas collects around the core.

Ice planets form even farther from the star, and there is more ice than rock dust. They have a tiny core and then a thick layer of slushy ice below just a thin wrapper of gas. The lightest gases, hydrogen and helium, don't freeze even this far from the star.

**Uranus** has a very faint ring system, but it looks as if its rings go top to bottom. They don't—Uranus was knocked over long ago in its history, so its north and south poles are now on the sides!

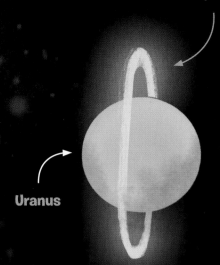

**Neptune**

**Uranus**

**ICE GIANTS**

## Hot ice!

The ice in a gas or ice planet isn't cold like the ice in your freezer. It's a hot, slushy solid, because the particles are crammed so close together they can't move around as they do in a liquid or gas.

**Saturn** has a set of rings around it that are made of millions of small, circling chunks of ice, rock, and dust.

# NASTY WEATHER

Gas giants are wracked by storms tearing through their upper atmosphere. Some storms last for hundreds of years. The "great red spot" on Jupiter is a storm that has been raging for 200 years or more. It's nearly one-and-a-half times the size of Earth and its winds whip round at 432 kph (268 mph).

## No surface

On gas planets, the gas just gets thicker and thicker toward the middle until it becomes first a liquid, and finally a kind of thick slushy ice. The core of a gas planet is much larger than Earth, but still tiny compared to the whole planet. If you traveled into a gas giant, the gas would eventually become so dense that you wouldn't be able to move through it any more.

# MAKING MOONS

Many planets have moons. In our solar system, rocky planets have few moons, but the gas giants have many. There are lots of different designs of moon!

## Moons—it's natural

A moon is a "natural satellite" of a planet—it's something which orbits a planet and has come about naturally. Earth has artificial satellites, too. They are objects we have launched into space to go around Earth, such as the International Space Station.

## Catch a falling moon

Some planets trap a moon as it passes. If an asteroid strays too close to a planet, gravity can drag it into orbit and it becomes a moon.

## Moon gallery

Our solar system has masses of moons, from huge to tiny, and from regular to truly weird. Meet a few of our best moons.

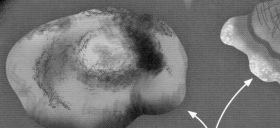

**Atlas**
30 km (18.7 miles) across, orbiting Saturn .

Pan and Atlas have a bulge around the middle where dust from Saturn's rings has stuck to them.

**Pan**
28 km (17.4 miles) across, orbiting Saturn.

**Prometheus**
136 km (85 miles) long, orbiting Saturn.

**Mimas**
396 km (246 miles) across, orbiting Saturn, Mimas s the smallest properly round moon. It has a massive crater from an asteroid smash.

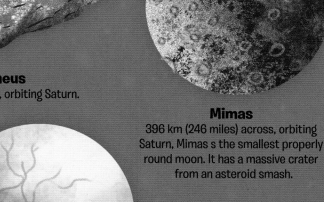

**Enceladus**
500 km (310 miles) across, orbiting Saturn, Enceladus is entirely covered with ice, but water erupts from a sub-surface ocean through ice volcanoes.

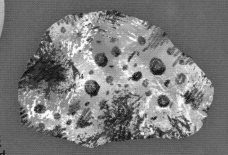

**Phoebe**
213 km (132 miles) across, orbiting Saturn, Phoebe is very dark and heavily cratered. It's probably a captured comet.

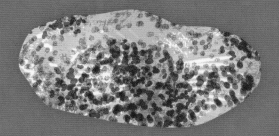

## Hyperion
410 km (255 miles) long, orbiting Saturn, is lighter than water and might be just a pile of rubble.

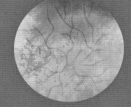

## Europa
3,100 km (1,940 miles) across, orbiting Jupiter, has an ice shell 15–25 km (10–15 miles) thick floating on an ocean 60–150 km (40–100 miles) deep. It's the most likely place besides Earth to host life.

## Callisto
4,820 km (2,995 miles) across, orbiting Jupiter, Callisto has the oldest and most heavily cratered surface in the solar system.

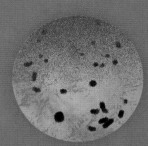

## Io
3,643 km (2,264 miles) across, orbiting Jupiter, Io is the most volcanically active world in the solar system. Its solid ground has tides and moves five times as much as Earth's ocean tides.

## Ganymede
5,268 km (3,273 miles) across, orbiting Jupiter is the largest moon—larger than the planet Mercury.

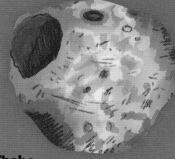

## Thebe
116 km (72 miles) across, orbiting Jupiter, Thebe is made mostly of water ice and has a massive crater at one end.

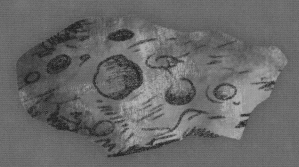

## Amalthea
250 km (155 miles) long, orbiting Jupiter, is probably made of ice and rubble.

## Make your own moon
Some planets form with moons right from the start. They grow from the same mix of rocks, dust, and gas that build the planet. And some moons are made with the debris from a giant collision when something crashes into the planet.

## Around and around
A moon turns on its own axis as well as going around a planet. As it spins, gravity pulls all parts of it toward the middle, which tends to make it round. Not all moons have enough mass to become round.

# LEFTOVERS

Lots of bits and pieces were left over from building the planets of our solar system. Hundreds of protoplanets hurtled around the Sun, smashing into each other, breaking apart and regrouping. In the end, there were eight planets left, and a huge number of chunks of rock and ice. Some of the lumps became moons, and others just stayed as chunks in orbit around the Sun.

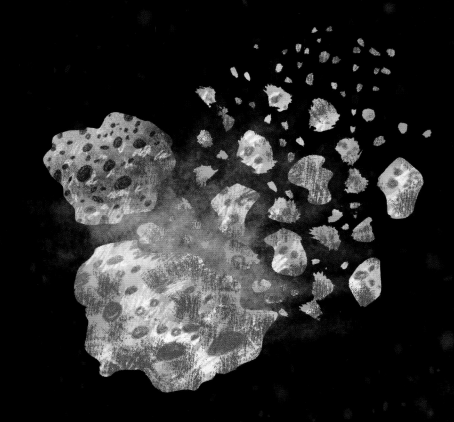

Pluto

## Planets that didn't make it

Some large rocky chunks aren't big enough to qualify as full planets, but are called "dwarf planets." They are roughly round, and some have moons, but if they haven't gathered up all the dust and rocks in their path around the Sun, or if their orbit isn't circular, they don't count as full planets. The most famous dwarf planet is Pluto. It was counted as a planet until 2006 when the rules changed.

An asteroid (**Ida**) with its own moon (**Dactyl**)

Pluto compared to Earth

## All together

A lot of the rocky chunks orbit in a great band between Mars and Jupiter, called the Asteroid Belt. They range from tiny specks to Ceres, 946 km (588 miles) across. These lumps are called asteroids. They are pieces that didn't manage to form into a planet, or debris from protoplanets that have been smashed in collisions.

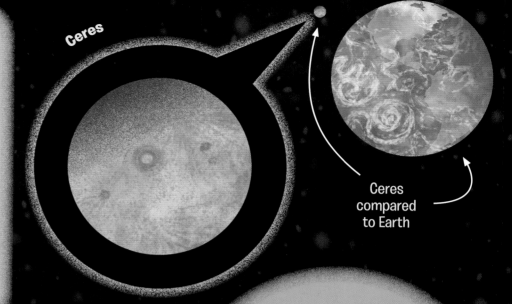

Ceres

Ceres compared to Earth

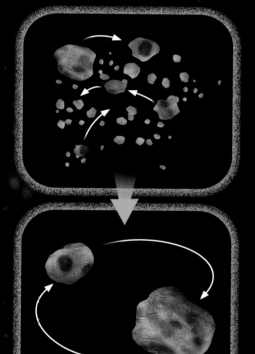

Arrokoth

## Raw ingredients

Asteroids contain the ingredients of the solar system, completely unchanged over 4.6 billion years. Most stay in the Asteroid Belt, but every now and then one is forced out and goes hurtling through space. When they fall to Earth, they are called meteorites. Meteorites enable scientists to study the make-up of the solar system in its very earliest days.

## ASTEROIDS ON COLLISION COURSE

A huge asteroid smashed into Earth 66 million years ago, killing nearly three quarters of the types of plants and animals living on Earth at that time, including all the dinosaurs except birds. Birds are the last surviving descendants of the dinosaurs.

## Far out

Not all the spare chunks are circling around in the Asteroid Belt. Some are much farther from the Sun. Pluto is beyond Neptune, on the edge of another, larger, band of leftover lumps called the Kuiper Belt. The most distant object a spaceship has visited is Arrokoth in the Kuiper Belt. Just 22 km (14 miles) long, it's made of two asteroids that have joined and stuck together. It's more than 40 times as far from the Sun as Earth is.

# COMETS AND OTHER CHUNKS

While asteroids are rocky bits that didn't become rocky planets, comets are icy objects that didn't become ice planets. Comets are ice with a bit of rock dust; asteroids are rock with a bit of ice. Although we call them different things, there is really no clear boundary—there is a full range of mixes of ice and rock.

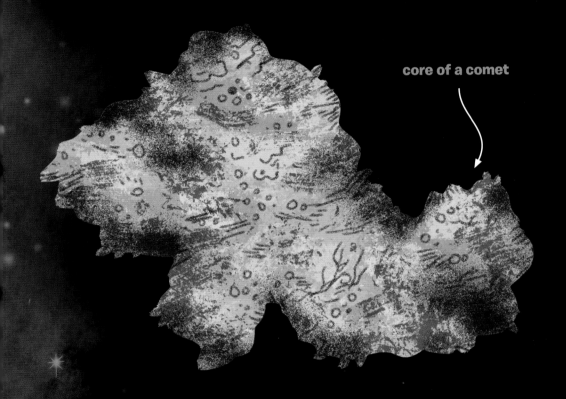

core of a comet

### Dirty snowballs

Comets are like "dirty snowballs," made mostly of ice with bits of rocky dust stuck in them. The ice is not all only water ice, but other substances that can freeze solid far out in space, including substances that are gases when nearer the Sun. We see them when they come near the Sun, and gain glittering tails that trail behind them.

### Even more far out

Comets spend most of their time far out in the cold Kuiper Belt, or even beyond it in an area called the Oort Cloud. The Oort Cloud is a huge spherical shell of icy lumps wrapped around the solar system. It's unimaginably vast—it starts 2,000 times as far from the Sun than Earth does and it ends 200,000 times as far away. There's space for trillions of comets.

Comets come back past the Sun again and again, shrinking a little each time. Some return quite often, but others have an orbit of thousands or even millions of years. Those from the Kuiper Belt come back in less than 200 years. Those from the Oort Cloud are rare visitors.

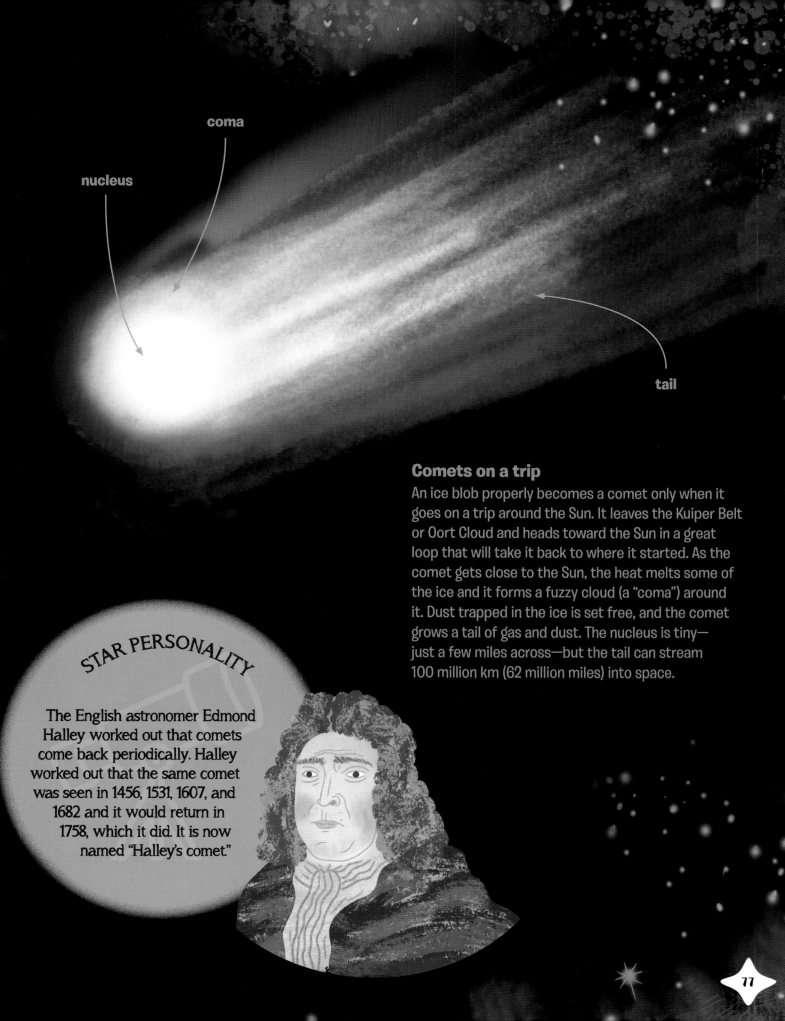

coma

nucleus

tail

## Comets on a trip

An ice blob properly becomes a comet only when it goes on a trip around the Sun. It leaves the Kuiper Belt or Oort Cloud and heads toward the Sun in a great loop that will take it back to where it started. As the comet gets close to the Sun, the heat melts some of the ice and it forms a fuzzy cloud (a "coma") around it. Dust trapped in the ice is set free, and the comet grows a tail of gas and dust. The nucleus is tiny— just a few miles across—but the tail can stream 100 million km (62 million miles) into space.

## STAR PERSONALITY

The English astronomer Edmond Halley worked out that comets come back periodically. Halley worked out that the same comet was seen in 1456, 1531, 1607, and 1682 and it would return in 1758, which it did. It is now named "Halley's comet."

# A PLANET TO CALL OUR OWN

Earth is just one of trillions of planets in the universe, but it is our own planet—our home. It is the only planet we know of that has life of any kind. It's also the planet we know most about and can explore most easily. By investigating Earth, we not only learn more about our own planet, how it has formed, and how it works, but also how other planets might form and what they might be like. Some planets orbiting other stars are likely to be similar to the planets of our solar system, but there might also be some very different types of planets we know nothing about.

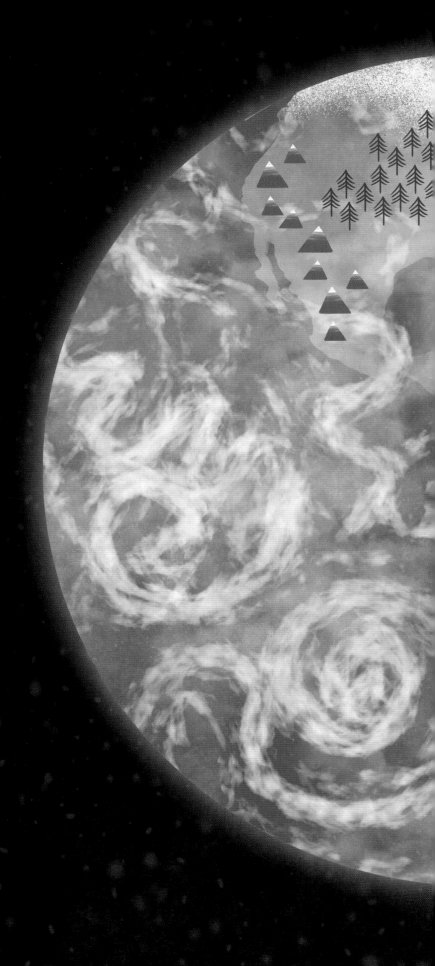

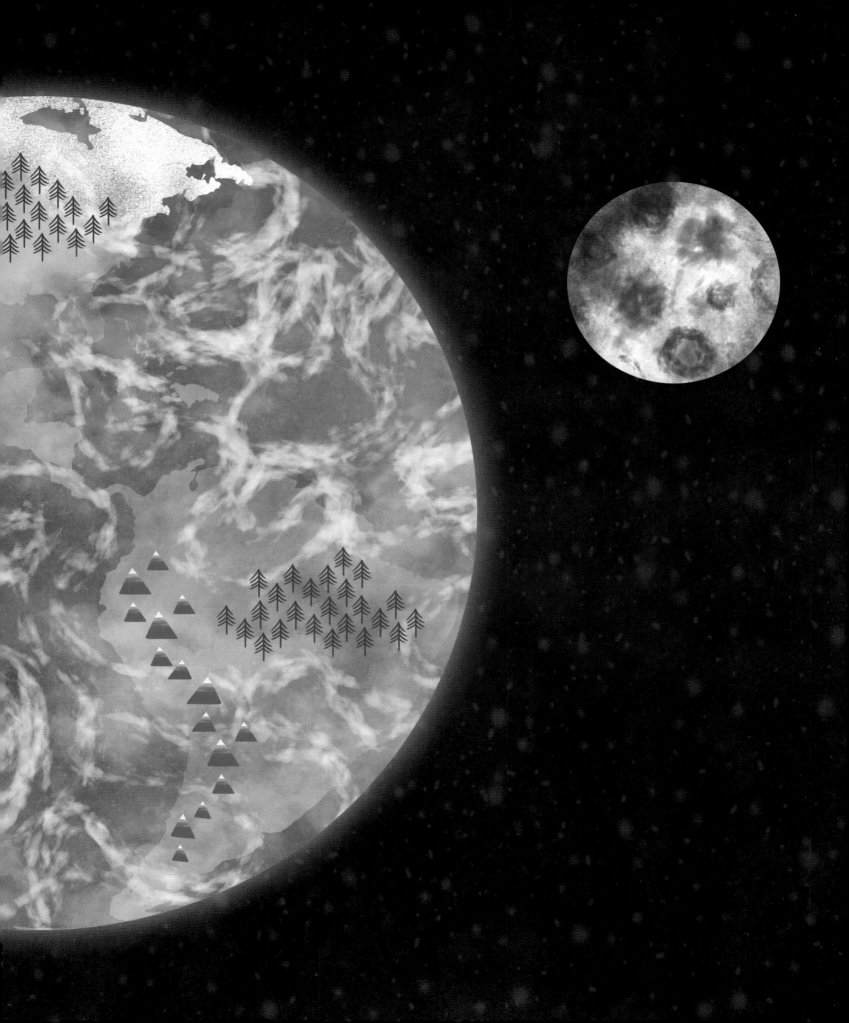

As the chunks of rock that made up Earth came together they grew hotter and hotter. Gravity crushed them together, heating them, until at last Earth melted. It was a vast ball of scalding molten rock, whirling in space.

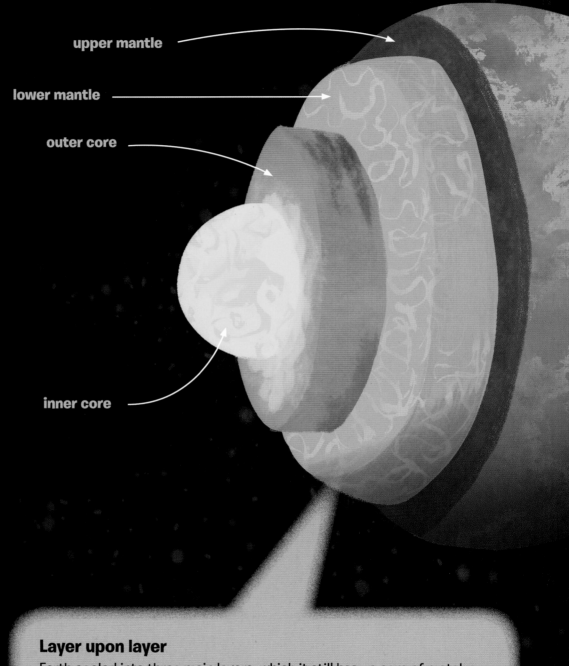

upper mantle

lower mantle

outer core

inner core

## All sorted

When Earth was molten, the metal, which was the heaviest part, could sink slowly to the middle. It eventually made a metal core. The rock was lighter and was not pulled as strongly inward. The core was wrapped in a thick envelope of hot, molten rock (the mantle).

In the cold of space, the rocky outside began to harden, making a crispy crust. Even as the rock started to solidify, the metal was still molten and could creep through cracks to the middle.

As Earth cooled, the lighter rock rose to the top of the mantle and hardened, while heavier rock sank lower and stayed molten. Some of the lighter rock was pulled back down and re-melted. But slowly, over time, Earth grew a crust of rock—solid ground.

## Layer upon layer

Earth cooled into three main layers, which it still has—a core of metal, a mantle of gooey, hot rock called magma, and a thin crust of hard rock.

The metal core is partly solid and partly liquid, even now. The very middle is as hot as the surface of the Sun, but the atoms are packed so tightly together that they can't move, so it's solid.

**crust**

# IN THE GREENHOUSE

Carbon dioxide is a greenhouse gas. That means it traps heat near the surface of the planet. With a lot of carbon dioxide in the atmosphere, a planet heats up. Venus has so much carbon dioxide that the surface is scorching hot and nothing can live there, but until 700 million years ago, it was probably cool enough to have liquid water and could even have supported some kind of life.

## Bad air days

Above the crust is a blanket of gases: Earth's atmosphere. Earth first had a layer of gases trapped from the solar nebula, mostly hydrogen and helium. Those gases were light, and were lost to space early on. Earth grew a new atmosphere from gases that leaked out of the mantle. Over millions of years, gas rose up through the mantle and crust as bubbles and collected above the surface.

One of the gases was water, so hot that it was a gas. Eventually, this water would make the oceans. The rest of the gas was mostly carbon dioxide, which kept Earth warm.

**Venus**

Volcanoes bring gases and molten rock from deep within a planet. Volcanoes on early Earth helped to build our planet's oceans and atmosphere.

# A LONELY MOON

The gas and ice giants have many moons each, but the rocky planets have few—
Mars has just two, and Mercury and Venus don't have any at all.
Earth is the only planet with just one moon. Our planet came
by its solitary Moon in a terrible accident!

Sun

## Make your own moon

Earth didn't form with a moon. Our Moon was
created in a massive collision between our planet and
a proto-planet about the size of Mars, called Theia. The
catastrophic crash happened when Earth was only 100 million
years old. Theia might have formed in an orbit that crossed Earth's path, or perhaps
was knocked into Earth's orbit. A crash was bound to happen sooner or later.

Theia was far bigger than the Moon, but about half the size of Earth. The crash
would have been so violent that Theia and a lot of Earth would have vaporized—
turned instantly to gas. A cloud of rock-gas circled Earth until it condensed
(solidified) into rock. The pieces of rock would have slowly grouped together,
in just the same way as the rocky planets formed in the first place.

Earth

## No more Theia

Theia was completely destroyed in the smash. Some of its
vaporized rock would have mixed with vaporized bits of
Earth to make the Moon, and some would have mixed into
the molten surface of Earth. Earth and the Moon are made
of similar material—a mix of early Earth and Theia.

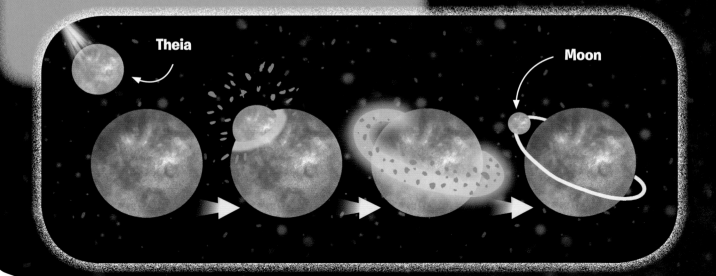

Theia

Moon

Theia

## EARTH'S NEW NOT-A-MOON

Occasionally, Earth gets a new companion, an extra "quasi-satellite." It has one now. These nearly moons loop around Earth, sharing our orbit for hundreds of years before drifting away. The current nearly moon is just 91 m (300 ft) long. It's been here for 100 years and will hang around for a few more centuries.

## More bumps and scratches

Asteroid strikes didn't end with the Moon-making collision. All the rocky planets—and the new Moon— were bombarded by big and small rocks from space for a very long time. We can see the craters on the Moon that these crashes created. A layer of dust, called "regolith" covers the surface of the Moon. This has been made by crashing asteroids smashing apart and also breaking up the Moon's rocky surface.

# SEA AND ROCK

**Earth's seas came from deep inside the planet. The water that clung to the chunks of rock that got together to form Earth made its way to the surface along with the bubbles of other gases that made up the atmosphere. This water eventually made oceans that covered most of the planet—Earth became a world of water and rock.**

## Wet from within

Water came out of the magma as a gas and collected in the atmosphere. While the surface of Earth was still hot enough to boil water, this water stayed as gas. But when the air cooled enough for it to condense (turn liquid), it formed tiny droplets in the air. These droplets gathered into clouds, just as they do now. And then it rained. It rained and rained and rained. Over tens of millions of years, water collected on the surface of Earth, filling the dips in the hard rocks making first puddles, and then lakes, and finally, vast oceans. By four billion years ago, Earth had a watery surface, with islands of rock.

## The salt in the sea

Carbon dioxide from the atmosphere dissolved in the water and made it acidic. The water then dissolved minerals from the rocks, becoming salty—as it still is today. It doesn't get saltier and saltier, but stays about the same, even over billions of years.

## Hot rocks

There are three types of rocks. Igneous rocks are cooled magma (molten rock inside Earth), which comes out of volcanoes (extrusive) or hardens in the ground (intrusive). Earth's first crust was made entirely of igneous rock as magma cooled. Other kinds of rock came from this. Sedimentary rock is made when rock is crushed to sand or mud and squashed under great pressure. Metamorphic rock is made when igneous or sedimentary rock is heated until it bakes and changes.

**granite**
intrusive igneous rock

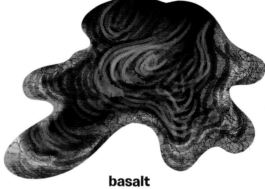

**basalt**
lava flow

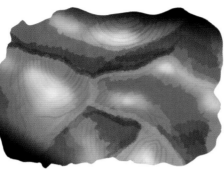

**basalt**
extrusive igneous rock

**sandstone**
sedimentary rock

**gneiss**
metamorphic rock

### SEE FOR YOURSELF

## ROCKS AROUND US

If you get the chance to collect stones on a beach, or go somewhere with exposed rocks, look at the patterns and shades in the rocks and pebbles. Sometimes water carrying dissolved minerals runs though gaps and cracks in rocks, leaving behind crystals that form stripes. Sometimes rocks of different types are pressed together and fused.

# LIVELY EARTH

The inside of Earth is still hot. The core is as hot as the surface of the Sun, but even the layer below the crust, the mantle, is still warm and gooey enough to flow very slowly. The crust is broken into chunks, called tectonic plates. Currents in the magma drag the plates around, and where plates meet, at boundaries or faults, Earth is active. It is still changing.

tectonic plate

fault

crust

mantle

core

## Spitting fire

Where there are breaks in the crust, hot magma can well up, rising to the surface (where it is called lava). In the middle of the oceans, the plates pull apart and magma leaks gently from the gap. It cools and hardens under the sea to make new rock that piles up. On land, magma pours from volcanoes, or is hurled out in dramatic and dangerous eruptions. Scalding lava, searing hot gases, and clouds of ash pour onto the surrounding land. Volcanoes can destroy cities or blast apart entire islands.

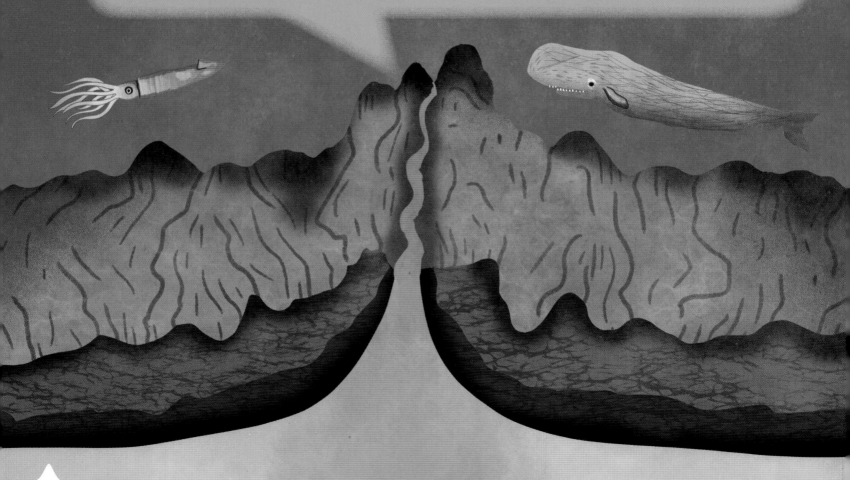

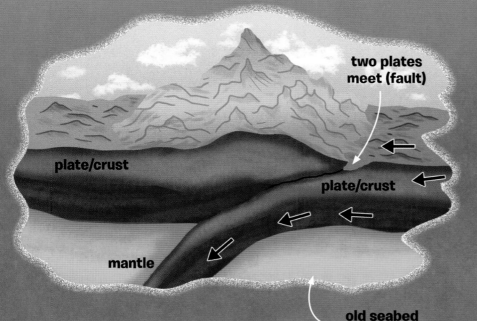

two plates meet (fault)

plate/crust

plate/crust

mantle

old seabed pulled down

## Shaking ground

Where two plates grind alongside each other, they often get stuck. Tension builds up along the edges of the plates where they try to move but catch on each other. Then they suddenly lurch when they get unjammed and the ground shakes and even cracks in an earthquake. Earthquakes in cities are dangerous, with falling buildings and bridges, roads breaking apart, and destroyed power and gas lines starting fires.

## Making and breaking continents

While new seabed is made in the middle of the oceans, old seabed is pulled down into the mantle near the coast and remelted. It feeds volcanoes along the edge of the land.

As the ocean widens, the plates carrying the land slowly move around. Over hundreds of millions of years, the continents come together and break apart, changing shape and moving around the world from hot to cold areas and back again. Sometimes land makes a single large continent, then this breaks up. Eventually, the pieces come back together, making another, different super-continent.

ridge

ocean

trench

trench

land

mantle

inner core

outer core

SEE FOR YOURSELF

# MOVING LANDS

If you look at a map you can see that the shape of Africa fits the eastern coastline of North and South America. Long ago, these lands were joined together. Then the Atlantic Ocean opened up, pushing them apart. The Atlantic Ocean is still growing wider, at about the same speed as your fingernails grow.

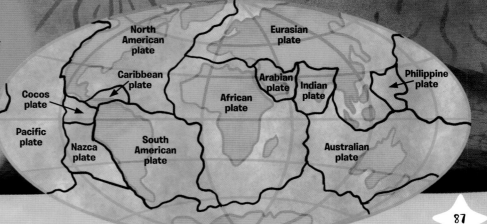

North American plate

Eurasian plate

Caribbean plate

Cocos plate

Arabian plate

Indian plate

Philippine plate

African plate

Pacific plate

Nazca plate

South American plate

Australian plate

# DRIFTING LANDS

The land has moved around over the face of Earth for between one and three billions years. This is called "continental drift." Sometimes the land is all clumped together in one vast supercontinent and other times, like now, it is broken up and spread out. Sometimes there is more land than there is now, and sometimes less. When it is warm, and there are no ice caps, sea levels rise. When it is cold, sea levels fall, revealing land that is currently underwater.

## STAR PERSONALITY

### Alfred Wegener

German weather researcher Alfred Wegener was fascinated by the way the coasts of South America and Africa seemed to fit together. He gathered evidence that these lands were once joined, and in 1912 he proposed a theory of continental drift—that the blocks of land move slowly around Earth.

**Approximately 900 million years ago (mya)**

The first large supercontinent was Rodinia. All the land on Earth was grouped together near the South Pole and the rest of the planet was covered with sea.

## Approximately 255 mya

The most recent supercontinent, Pangea, formed about 330 million years ago. With all the land grouped together, the middle of the continent was probably hot and dry, with mountains keeping most rain to the coastal areas.

## Approximately 200 mya

Pangaea began splitting into two large continents around the time that the dinosaurs roamed Earth. Some of the shapes of modern landmasses were emerging, but all the land was still on the same side of the globe.

## Approximately 150 mya

The land was still grouped together, with no Atlantic Ocean to separate North America from Europe or South America from Africa. India was an island that would later drift north to attach to Asia.

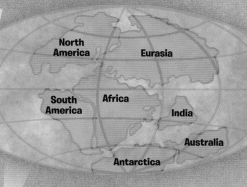

## Approximately 65 mya

By the time the dinosaurs died out, the Atlantic Ocean was beginning to form. The land was still fairly close together with one vast ocean on one side of the world.

## Present day

The modern landmasses are well separated. Australia and South America have separated from Antarctica, but India has joined to Asia, and North and South America are linked.

# LIFE STARTS

Scientists can't say exactly how or when life appeared on Earth, or even agree on what makes something "living." Perhaps just 100 million years after the Moon formed, or maybe a little later, chemicals that could copy themselves somehow crossed the line to become the first living things. Over time, they grew into single cells—tiny self-contained packages of living substance that used chemicals as food to grow and reproduce. Everything living on the planet now developed from those first organisms.

vesicle

## Insides and outsides

The smallest particles of matter are atoms. These can stick together into groups called molecules. Some molecules, called fatty acids, have one end that is attracted to water and one that is repelled (driven away) by water. In a pool of water, these molecules clump together with all the "water-hating" parts hiding together in the middle, and the "water-loving" parts on the outside. If these little balls—called micelles—collide, they can join together to make a bigger blob called a vesicle, which has two layers of molecules and a space in the middle. This space can hold water and other chemicals and keep it apart from the rest of the environment. These vesicles became the first cells, which are the basic building blocks of life. All living things have at least one cell—many have only one cell.

Micelle cross section

micelle

Vesicle cross section

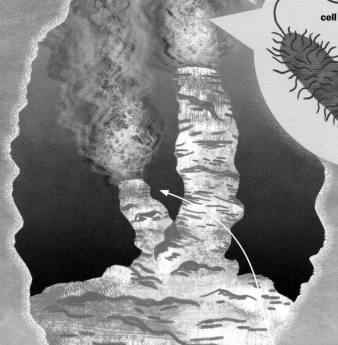

cell membrane

cell wall

cytoplasm

Archaea

## Ancient organisms

However the first life forms began, they led dull lives. They could feed on chemicals to give themselves energy, and they could reproduce, but they didn't do much else. These first organisms were called archaea. Early archaea left chemical "footprints" in the oldest rocks on Earth, telling us life began at least 3.8 billion years ago. Modern archaea give us an idea of what they might have been like. They are tiny, with a length less than a tenth of the thickness of a human hair. Many live in scorching temperatures, including in the near-boiling water in undersea vents, many live deep in the mud, and others live in the guts of cows and termites. They "eat" chemicals to make methane (the gas we use for heating and cooking). Conditions on early Earth would have suited them just fine.

undersea vents

## Life from light

Among the first single-celled life-forms, some learned to use energy from sunlight to break up chemicals and make sugars to feed themselves. They took in carbon dioxide from the atmosphere and released oxygen into the air. Plants still do this; it's called "photosynthesis." Although this set the planet on course for how it is now, it was a disaster at the time. Most of the life-forms didn't use oxygen. In fact, it poisoned them. As the photosynthesizing organisms (called cyanobacteria) increased and poured oxygen into the water and the air, lots of the other organisms were killed off by it. Around 2.4–2 billion years ago, the atmosphere changed, and life changed as a result. New organisms took over which could use—or at least put up with—oxygen.

## HOW DO WE KNOW?

Rocks from 2.5–2 billion years ago often have bright red stripes that are made by rust. The rust is iron oxide— a mix of iron and oxygen. It formed when cyanobacteria poured so much oxygen into the water that it rusted the iron in the sea and dropped it to be built into the rocks.

## Bigger and better

After a billion years or so, more exciting organisms developed. They still all lived in the sea, but they began to grow into larger plants and animals. They were the first living things that could be seen without a microscope—if anyone had been around to see them. Life took off, and by 500 million years ago was richly varied.

**400 million years ago**

# LIFE ON LAND

Imagine a land of rock, with nothing growing on it except perhaps some slime, but the shore is lapped by the tides. Earth was like that for billions of years. And then, about 700–550 million years ago, it began to change. Life came to land. At first, just lichen grew on the rocks, but then plants began to grow, and animals crawled from the seas and rivers.

## Don't forget your sunscreen!

A layer of a gas called ozone collected high up in the atmosphere. It protected Earth from the same damaging rays in sunlight that cause sunburn. Before that, the only safe place to live was in the water. But with Earth's sunscreen in place, life could come out in the open. It began with lichen that could cling to bare rock. Lichen are algae and a fungus living together.

## Taking root

The first things to grow on land didn't have roots. The lichen broke up the rock surface, and as the tiny organisms died, they added to the rock dust. This collected in dips and nooks and crannies of the rocks making the first soil. With soil, plants could grow roots. They crept farther from the shore and spread inland. Roots held soil in place—more plants meant more soil, and more soil meant more plants.

fishapod

92

## Feet following

With simple plants growing and the damaging sunlight filtered, animals could make their move onto land. The first to crawl from the sea were arthropods. Arthropods have hard, jointed outsides. They are animals like crabs, insects and spiders. They would have scuttled over the rocks, eating bits of plants—and each other. As they grew and changed, some insects took to the air, becoming the first-ever flying animals. Animal bodies and droppings added to the soil.

## PIONEERS

The next change came with eggs with a waterproof outside. These eggs could be laid on land. The animals that laid them, the reptiles, were freed from water and could live anywhere. Life had truly moved onto land.

## Fish out of water

Next, strange fish with stiffened, prop-like fins dragged themselves from the water. These odd "fishapods" could breathe air and were adapted to both land and sea. They evolved into the first amphibians: animals that can live on land but lay their eggs in water.

Plants, soil, and animals all spread farther in land, growing and changing, until 350 million years ago, towering tropical forests hummed with dragonflies the size of birds and crocodile-like amphibians lumbered through hot swamps.

**giant dragonfly**

**arthropods**

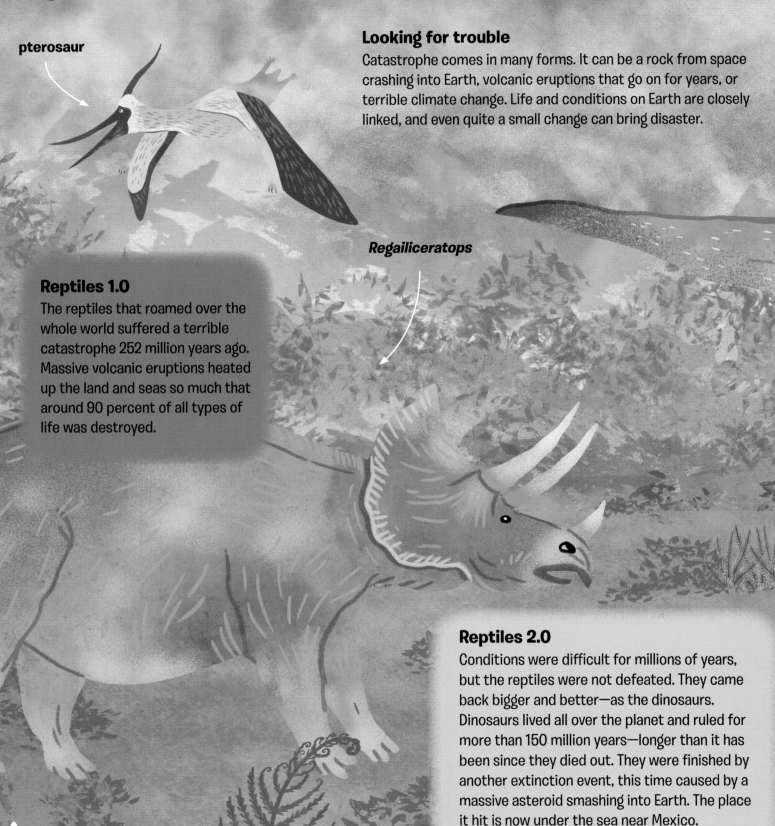

# MASS EXTINCTIONS

**Life was going really nicely—until suddenly it wasn't. At least five times in the past, most living things have been wiped out in a mass extinction event, when most organisms die.**

pterosaur

## Looking for trouble

Catastrophe comes in many forms. It can be a rock from space crashing into Earth, volcanic eruptions that go on for years, or terrible climate change. Life and conditions on Earth are closely linked, and even quite a small change can bring disaster.

*Regailiceratops*

## Reptiles 1.0

The reptiles that roamed over the whole world suffered a terrible catastrophe 252 million years ago. Massive volcanic eruptions heated up the land and seas so much that around 90 percent of all types of life was destroyed.

## Reptiles 2.0

Conditions were difficult for millions of years, but the reptiles were not defeated. They came back bigger and better—as the dinosaurs. Dinosaurs lived all over the planet and ruled for more than 150 million years—longer than it has been since they died out. They were finished by another extinction event, this time caused by a massive asteroid smashing into Earth. The place it hit is now under the sea near Mexico.

## Room for the rest

Mass extinctions are terrible for the animals and plants living at the time. Conditions change and survival becomes a struggle. Both volcanic eruptions and an asteroid strike throw dust and gas into the air, blocking the Sun and cooling the planet. Later it heats up, baking anything that has survived. Plants die, and then the animals that eat plants die, and then the animals that eat the plant-eaters die. But slowly life recovers. With so many types gone, new animals and plants move into the gaps. They adapt to the conditions, and use the spaces and types of food they can find. After the dinosaurs, little animals that had been lurking underground or scampering through the trees took over. They were the mammals.

*Tyrannosaurus rex*

*Ankylosaurus*

## HOW DO WE KNOW?

We know about life from the past because some dead animals and plants are preserved as fossils. If they are buried quickly in mud or sludge, the hard parts of their bodies can change chemically, becoming like rock. Scientists can piece their bones, shells, claws, teeth, and beaks back together to work out what they were like. They can tell from the rocks they are found in how long ago they lived.

# ON TO US

Life bounces back after extinction events. With the dinosaurs reduced to just the ancestors of modern birds, there was space for new kinds of organisms. Mammals rose to fill many of the gaps left by the dinosaurs. And among mammals, humans to rose to rule Earth.

gibbon

## Warm blood and big brains

Mammals have several features that helped them to succeed. They are warm-blooded, which means they can control their own body temperature, so they can live in hot or cold places without overheating or freezing. They protect their young, growing them inside their own bodies and producing milk for them after they are born. And some mammals developed larger brains than previous types of animal. Among those are the primates, a group which includes all types of monkeys and apes, including humans.

bonobo

## Out of the trees

Primates first lived in the trees, but some began to spend more time on the forest floor and then the plains. Early humans and some other apes began to walk upright on two legs. Most had a thumb (and, except humans, a toe-thumb as well!), which means they could grasp objects easily—and that would come in very handy.

**Homo ergaster**
(HOH-moh er-GASS-tuhr)

**Homo habilis**
(HOH-moh HAH-bih-liss)

**Homo heidelbergensis**
(HOH-moh HY-duhl-burg-EN-siss)

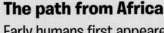

## The path from Africa

Early humans first appeared in Africa. There were several different types for a long time. The first modern humans appeared 200,000 years ago and left Africa around 50,000 years ago. They spread around the world, ending up last of all in North and then South America.

## From cave to city

Early humans learned to make tools, to fashion clothes and make fire. These last two meant they could move into areas that were colder than their thin coat of hair alone would allow. It meant the humans could spread everywhere.

In less than 20,000 years, humans went from living in caves, and getting food by hunting animals and collecting plants, to building homes, and farming plants and animals. This has meant we can share out tasks and even embark on projects that can't be finished in a single lifetime. That's allowed us to build huge cities, and develop science, arts and religions that grow over generations. Humans are the only species on Earth that have done anything like this. Our science and technology have made it possible to explore space and find out about the universe around us.

The Ishtar gate in the ancient city of Babylon, built 2,600 years ago.

# DISCOVERING SPACE

Humans are the only life form in the solar system that has begun to explore the universe (as far as we know). People have been fascinated by the night sky and the regular movements of the Sun, Moon and planets for thousands of years. At first, we could just track them as dots of light in the sky, and trace patterns made by the stars. Now, we have technology to help us look at objects far away in space. And with space travel, we can even visit some places in our solar system. Humans have visited the Moon, "walked" in space, and sent robotic spacecraft to other planets.

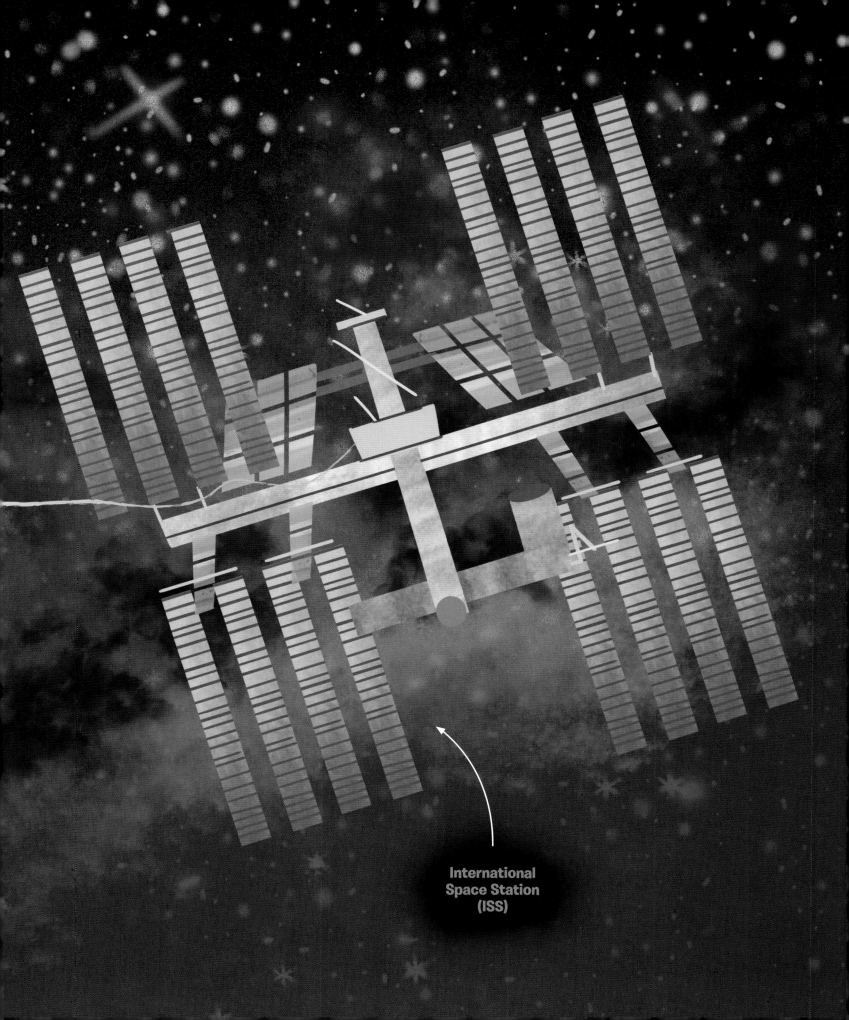

International
Space Station
(ISS)

# SEEING STARS

People have noticed and tracked the phases of the Moon and movements of the planets, and recorded the positions of the stars since ancient times. Although some other animals seem to use the Moon and Sun to find their way, humans are the only species to study astronomy and explore space.

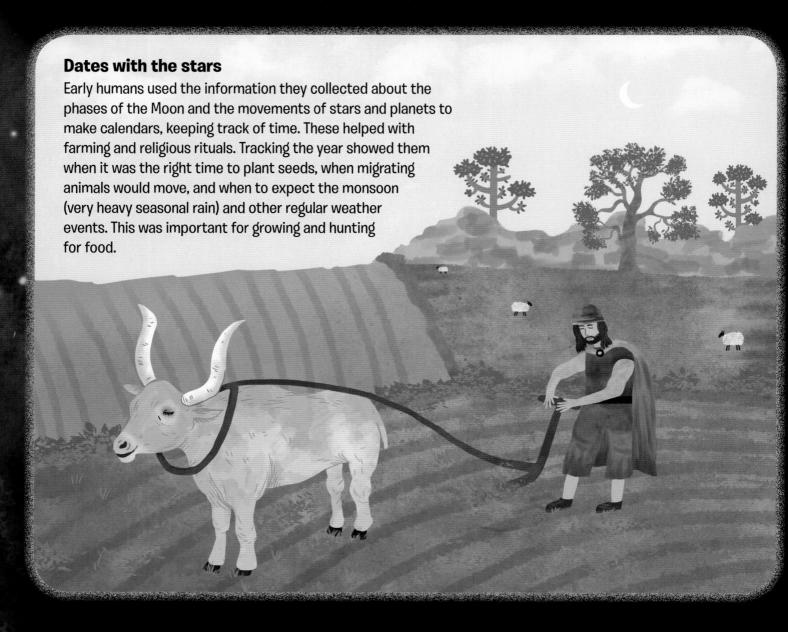

## Dates with the stars

Early humans used the information they collected about the phases of the Moon and the movements of stars and planets to make calendars, keeping track of time. These helped with farming and religious rituals. Tracking the year showed them when it was the right time to plant seeds, when migrating animals would move, and when to expect the monsoon (very heavy seasonal rain) and other regular weather events. This was important for growing and hunting for food.

People in many early societies believed events in the heavens affected events on Earth, developing ideas of astrology. In fact, events like eclipses and the appearance of comets have no effect on our lives or on events such as wars and food shortages.

People have associated the planets and stars with gods in many places and ages. Even though we no longer share these beliefs, the data these people collected about the movement of the objects in the sky laid the foundations for astronomy.

## Sailing by the stars

For thousands of years, people have used the position of the stars to navigate (find their way) at night, and the position of the Sun to navigate by day and to tell the time. For this to work, they needed to keep detailed records of the positions of the stars over many years. The sky was darker in the past, as there was no light pollution from modern cities, so far more stars were visible. People could easily see the stars they needed to fix on to navigate the oceans.

## HOW DO WE KNOW?

Objects and monuments that have survived for thousands of years show that our distant ancestors took notice of the stars and planets. The monument Stonehenge in England is 5,000 years old. It has stones that are placed so that the rising Sun at the summer solstice (the longest day of the year) shines onto an important stone.

**Stonehenge**

# LOOKING AT THE STARS

To our ancestors, everything except the Sun and Moon looked like spots of light in the sky. The stars and planets moved differently, and stars twinkled, but there was no way to tell how different they were. Then, in 1608, a lens maker in Europe made the first telescope. That invention changed our understanding of the universe for ever.

## Seeing more

The telescope showed for the first time that the planets are other worlds in the solar system, and that the Milky Way is a massive band of stars, numbering countless millions. It revealed that the surface of the Moon has craters, mountains, and plains rather than being smooth and featureless, as people once thought. It even showed that some of the other planets in the solar system have moons of their own.

These discoveries changed people's view of themselves and their world. They supported the idea, suggested less than 100 years before, that Earth goes around the Sun rather than the Sun and all the planets going around Earth. If the planets were other worlds, perhaps they, too, were the home to living beings. People wondered what these other worlds were like and whether anything that lived there might look like us.

Moon

STAR PERSONALITY

## Galilei Galileo

The Italian scientist Galileo heard about the invention of the telescope and immediately made a much better one himself. Using it, he discovered the cratered surface of the Moon, that the Milky Way is a vast stripe of stars, and that the planets of the solar system are other worlds, not spots of light like the stars. He also saw the first four moons around another planet—Jupiter.

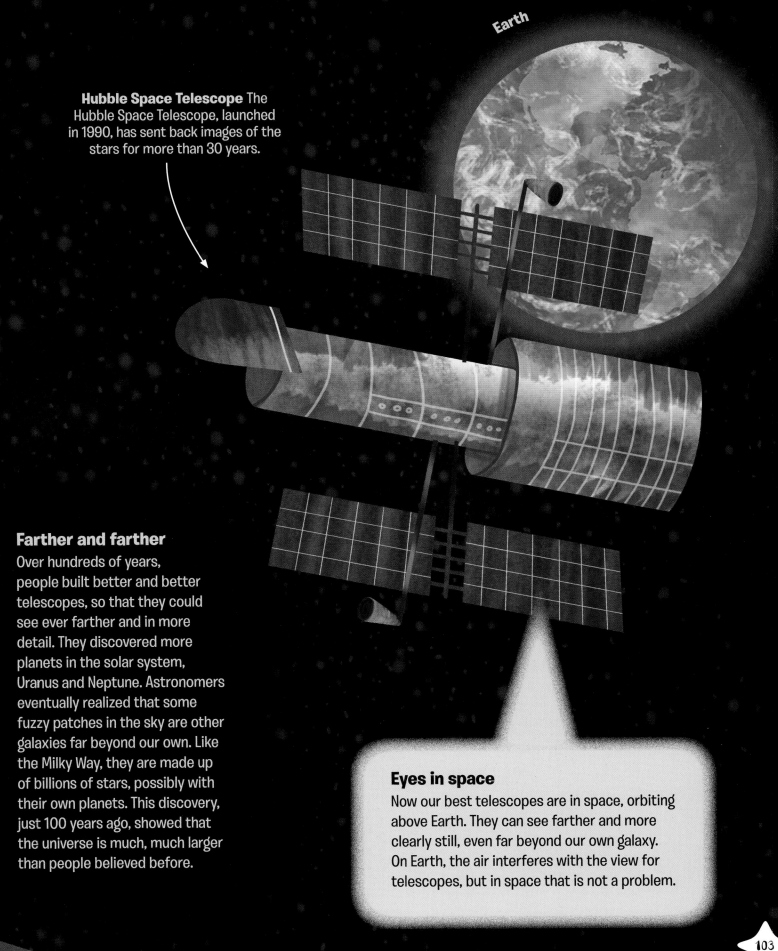

**Earth**

**Hubble Space Telescope** The Hubble Space Telescope, launched in 1990, has sent back images of the stars for more than 30 years.

## Farther and farther

Over hundreds of years, people built better and better telescopes, so that they could see ever farther and in more detail. They discovered more planets in the solar system, Uranus and Neptune. Astronomers eventually realized that some fuzzy patches in the sky are other galaxies far beyond our own. Like the Milky Way, they are made up of billions of stars, possibly with their own planets. This discovery, just 100 years ago, showed that the universe is much, much larger than people believed before.

## Eyes in space

Now our best telescopes are in space, orbiting above Earth. They can see farther and more clearly still, even far beyond our own galaxy. On Earth, the air interferes with the view for telescopes, but in space that is not a problem.

# MORE WAYS OF SEEING

Stars and other objects shine with light but also put out many other sorts of radiation. Modern telescopes can pick up some of these other types of radiation, such as radio waves, microwaves, and X-rays, and use them to investigate objects in space.

### Radio stars

The first simple radio telescope was made in 1931, but they have become much more advanced over the last 90 years. These telescopes are used with computers to produce images of what objects "look" like in radio or other types of radiation. They measure the amount of radiation of a certain type and make a map of how much there is at different points in the sky or around an object. The various levels are then shown in different shades to make a map that gives a visual idea of the object.

## HAPPY ACCIDENT

Engineer Karl Jansky picked up the first radio waves from space in 1932 by accident. He was looking for sources of interference on telephone lines when his radio antenna picked up a background hum. Eventually he worked out it came from space, somewhere near the middle of the Milky Way. Grote Reber made the first radio telescope (on purpose!) in 1937.

A radio telescope focuses on a particular path of sky.

It picks up radiation with a wavelength longer than visible light.

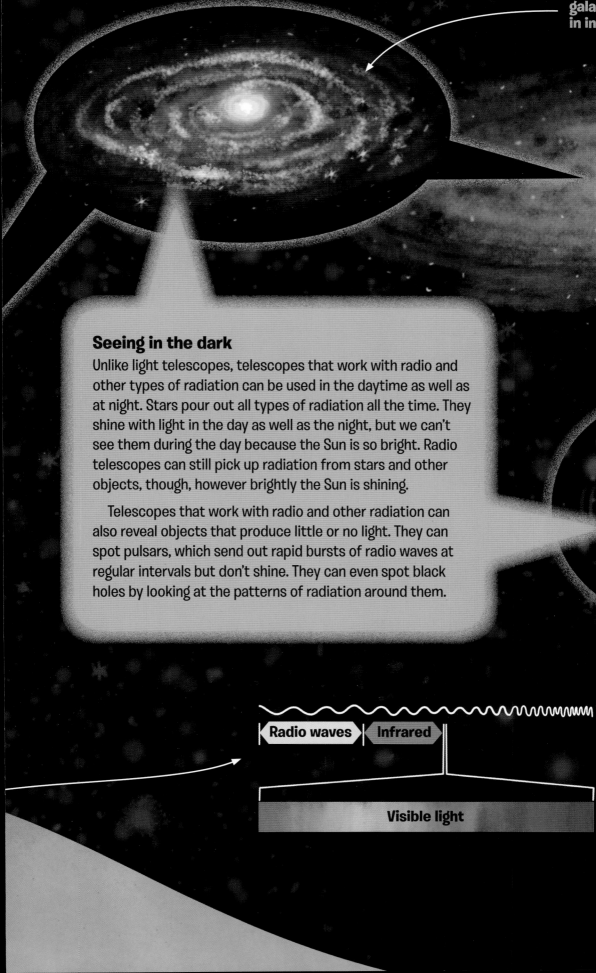

## Seeing in the dark

Unlike light telescopes, telescopes that work with radio and other types of radiation can be used in the daytime as well as at night. Stars pour out all types of radiation all the time. They shine with light in the day as well as the night, but we can't see them during the day because the Sun is so bright. Radio telescopes can still pick up radiation from stars and other objects, though, however brightly the Sun is shining.

Telescopes that work with radio and other radiation can also reveal objects that produce little or no light. They can spot pulsars, which send out rapid bursts of radio waves at regular intervals but don't shine. They can even spot black holes by looking at the patterns of radiation around them.

Radio waves    Infrared

Visible light

# WE HAVE LIFT OFF!

We can discover lots about space by using different kinds of telescopes, but since the middle of the twentieth century, we have had another way of exploring space. We can now send spacecraft to investigate other planets and moons in the solar system. It began with daring journeys in the 1960s, when humans first left the planet.

Sputnik
(Soviet
Union)

## The race for space

The first object to be blasted into space from Earth looked like a slightly small, silver basketball. The artificial satellite, called Sputnik, was launched in 1957 from the Soviet Union. It made one trip round Earth every 90 minutes—a total of 1,440 orbits during the thee months it worked.

Sputnik sparked a "space race" as the Soviet Union and the USA competed to achieve more and more in space. The Soviet Union put the first human into space in 1961, landed the first spacecraft on the Moon (1966), made the first space walk (1965), and first saw the far side of the Moon (1966). But the USA overtook the USSR in 1969 by landing two astronauts from Apollo 11 on the Moon.

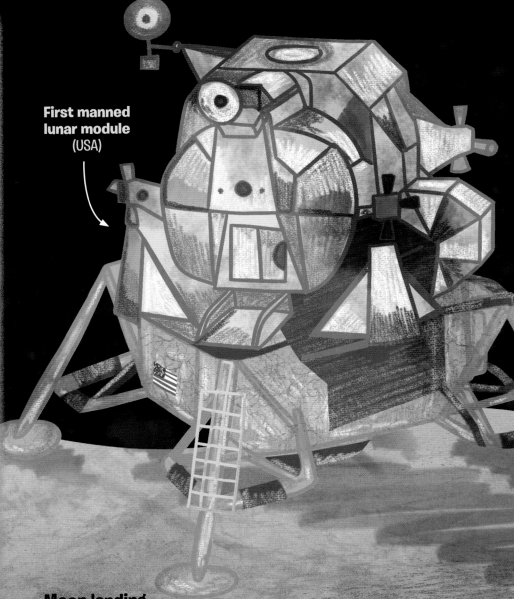

First manned
lunar module
(USA)

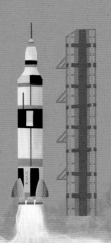

**Rocket launch**

## Moon landing

It was the first time that any living being from Earth had landed on another object in space. The astronauts took photos, made measurements, and collected rock and dust from the Moon. The samples of Moon rock tell us about the early solar system and the matter that Earth and the other planets are made of. The rocks are still being investigated, more than 50 years after they were collected.

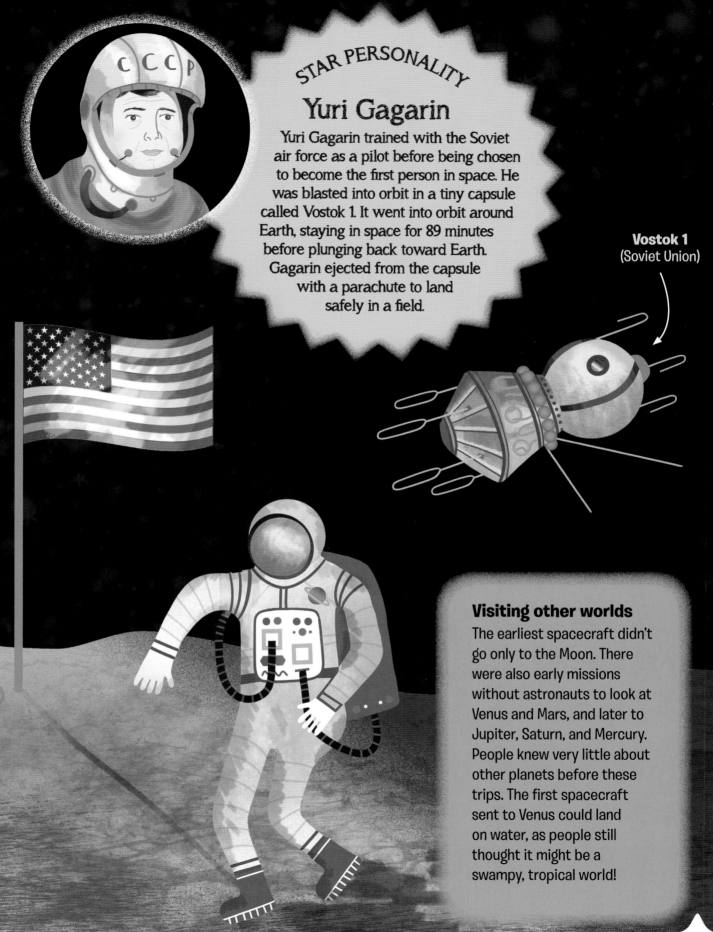

# Yuri Gagarin

Yuri Gagarin trained with the Soviet air force as a pilot before being chosen to become the first person in space. He was blasted into orbit in a tiny capsule called Vostok 1. It went into orbit around Earth, staying in space for 89 minutes before plunging back toward Earth. Gagarin ejected from the capsule with a parachute to land safely in a field.

**Vostok 1**
(Soviet Union)

## Visiting other worlds

The earliest spacecraft didn't go only to the Moon. There were also early missions without astronauts to look at Venus and Mars, and later to Jupiter, Saturn, and Mercury. People knew very little about other planets before these trips. The first spacecraft sent to Venus could land on water, as people still thought it might be a swampy, tropical world!

# ADVENTURES WITH ROBOTS

It's much easier and safer to send robotic spacecraft (probes) into space than to send astronauts. Robotic craft can travel for a very long time and don't need any food or air. They can withstand dangerous conditions and they don't miss home! Probes have revealed lots about the solar system that we could not have learned any other way.

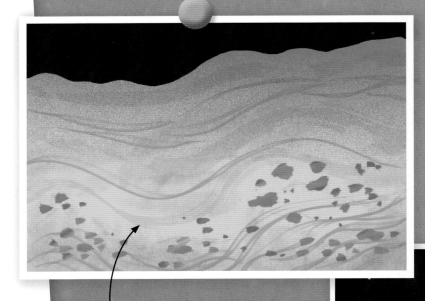

**Venus** has a scorching surface under an acidic, yellow sky.

**Mars** is covered with reddish dust and rocks, with craters.

**The Mars Curiosity rover** even took selfies while it roamed the surface of Mars!

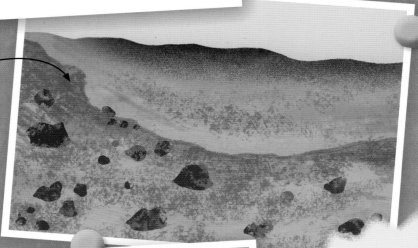

## STAR PERSONALITY

## Curiosity rover

The Mars Curiosity rover is the largest and most advanced rover ever sent to Mars. Since August 2012, Curiosity has been roving around a small area of the surface, collecting and examining interesting rocks. Its aim is to discover whether Mars could have once had the right conditions for life. It's about as tall as a basketball player and the size of a small car.

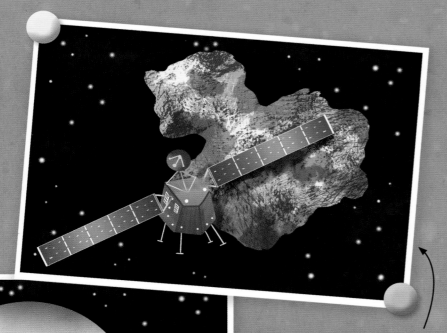

## Flybys and landings

Some probes travel through space to another planet or moon and orbit above it, collecting photos and making different types of measurement and observation. Others carry landers which can go down to the surface of a rocky planet and collect even more information. Some landers stay in one place, but others are "rovers" and can move around, collecting samples of dust and rock, taking photos, and making measurements in different places.

Not all probes and landers go to planets and moons. Some have visited comets and asteroids, and one has even returned a capsule of dust trapped from the tail of a comet.

**Rosetta** Rosetta approaching comet 67P/Churyumov-Gerasimenko where it dropped a lander, Philae, to study the comet's surface.

**The Cassini-Huygens probe** spent 13 years orbiting Saturn, studying the planet and its moons and ring system.

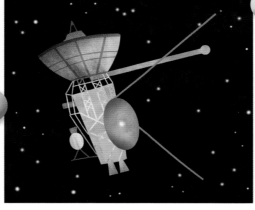

**Cassini** carried a lander called Huygens, which it released onto the moon Titan in 2005—the most distant landing so far.

The New Horizons probe sent back the first detailed photos of **Pluto** in 2015.

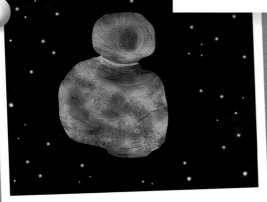

New Horizons went on to fly by **Arrokoth** in the Kuiper Belt in 2019. It is the most distant object explored.

## Keeping in touch

Probes send their information back to Earth using a radio link. It can include photographs and video footage, reports of the chemicals in the atmosphere or surface of a planet, and information about the temperature, magnetic field, or other conditions it finds.

# OUR SOLAR SYSTEM

Our solar system has eight planets, hundreds of moons, and billions of asteroids and comets. The variety of our planets gives us information about what types of planets might form around other stars, though different types that we don't have here are also possible.

**Asteroid belt**
Distance from Sun: 330–479 million km (204–297 million miles)
Number of objects: 1 million
Distance between objects: 965,600 km (600,000 miles)

**Sun**
Radius (from middle to edge): 695,700 km (432,288 miles).

**Venus**
Type: Rocky
Radius: 6,052 km (3,783 miles)
Day: 2,802 hours
Year: 225 Earth days
Moons: 0
Distance from Sun: 108 million km (68 million miles)

**Earth**
Type: Rocky
Radius: 6,378 km (3,986 miles)
Day: 24 hours
Year: 365 days
Moons: 1
Distance from Sun: 150 million km (93.5 million miles)

**Mercury**
Type: Rocky
Radius: 2,440 km (1,525 miles)
Day: 4,223 hours
Year: 88 Earth days
Moons: 0
Distance from Sun: 58 million km (36 million miles)

**Mars**
Type: Rocky
Radius: 3,396 km (2,123 miles)
Day: 25 hours
Year: 687 Earth days
Moons: 2
Distance from Sun: 228 million km (142 million miles)

## Uranus

**Type:** Ice giant
**Radius:** 24,764 km (15,473 miles)
**Day:** 16.1 hours
**Year:** 59,800 Earth days
**Moons:** 14
**Distance from Sun:** 4,495 million km (2,809 million miles)

## Neptune

**Type:** Ice giant
**Radius:** 25,559 km (15,974 miles)
**Day:** 17 hours
**Year:** 30,589 Earth days
**Moons:** 27
**Distance from Sun:** 2,872.5 million km (1,795 million miles)

## Saturn

**Type:** Gas giant
**Radius:** 60,268 km (37,668 miles)
**Day:** 11 hours
**Year:** 10,747 Earth days
**Moons:** 82
**Distance from Sun:** 1,433.5 million km (896 million miles)

## Jupiter

**Type:** Gas giant
**Radius:** 71,492 km (44,683 miles)
**Day:** 10 hours
**Year:** 4,331 Earth days
**Moons:** 79
**Distance from Sun:** 779 million km (487 million miles)

## Not to scale

The picture on this page doesn't show you how large the Sun, planets, and moons are compared to one another, nor does it show you how far apart they are. Neptune is 4.5 billion km (2.8 billion miles from the Sun). If the Sun were the size it is on this page, the picture of Earth would be just 2 mm (0.08 in) across and 21 m (70 ft) away. The picture of Neptune would be over 600 m (2000 ft) away.

# MATTER AND SPACE: FROM QUARKS TO GALAXIES

All matter is made of quarks and electrons, and they all came into existence in the first millionth of a second of space-time. Yet most of matter, from quarks to galaxies, is empty space. The tininess of quarks and the enormous size of galaxies and galaxy clusters is hard to get your head around.

## How small?

Quarks make up protons and neutrons, which form the nucleus of every atom. Hydrogen has a nucleus of just one proton made of three quarks. But there's so much empty space in the proton that it's 1,000–2,000 as far across as a single quark.

If this dot was a quark, the hydrogen nucleus would be nearly as far across as you are tall. In fact, about a trillion hydrogen nuclei could line up across that dot.

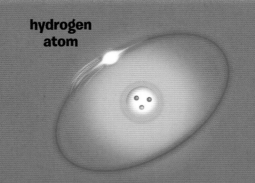

**hydrogen atom**

If a hydrogen nucleus was 1 cm (0.4 in) across, the electron would be up to 600 m (1,968 ft) away.

**nucleus**          **600 m**          **electron**

A hydrogen atom has one electron whizzing around its nucleus, but it's usually a long way away from the middle. A picture drawn to scale would be impossibly large, so illustrations show the electron near the nucleus.

But the hydrogen atom is still really small. If every person in the world was the size of a hydrogen atom and they stood in a line, the line would be only 80 cm long.

## Making matter

Atoms combine to make molecules. Some are small and simple, with just two or three atoms, like water and carbon dioxide. Some are giants, with thousands and thousands of atoms. But they are still too small to see.

Once molecules start getting together, there is no limit to the size things can grow. A tennis ball, an elephant, a mountain, a moon, a planet, a star—all are collections of molecules grouped in different ways. All could be broken down into atoms. Those atoms are made of protons, neutrons and electrons, the protons and neutrons made of quarks. Even a galaxy is made of quarks and electrons—and lots of empty space!

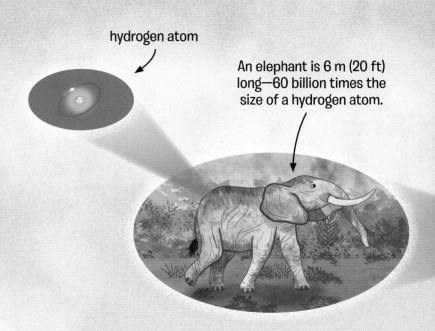

hydrogen atom

An elephant is 6 m (20 ft) long—60 billion times the size of a hydrogen atom.

Our galaxy is just one of at least 100 billion galaxies in the observable universe caption to come caption to come caption to come caption.

## DID YOU KNOW?

There are around $10^{80}$ atoms in the known universe—that's 1 followed by 80 zeroes.

The Milky Way is thought to be about 200,000 light years across. That's 50,000 times as wide as the solar system.

The solar system is about 4 light years across (about 4 trillion km, or 2.4 trillion miles). That's 625,000,000 times as wide as Earth.

Earth is nearly 6,400 km (4,000 miles) across—or 723 times as far across as Mount Everest is tall.

Mount Everest is nearly 8,850 m (29,000 ft) tall, which is 1,475 times as tall as an elephant is long.

# LOOKING FOR LIFE

The Milky Way has hundreds of billions of planets. Ours is probably not the only one with life, but we don't actually know about any life elsewhere. Scientists look at the conditions on Earth that have made life possible and hunt for similar conditions in the search for life in space.

**HABITABLE ZONE**
Life is most likely to be found where the temperature is right for water to be liquid.

too hot

**just right**
(Earth)

too cold

### Life or not?
It's impossible to tell how easy it is for life to start and keep going. Our planet seems to be the only one in the solar system with life, but life here started soon after the planet formed. That suggests it's quite easy for it to get going. It took four billion years to get a wide variety of advanced types of life, though. Maybe it's hard for life to progress.

## Living nearby?
Nowhere else in the solar system seems to have complex life like Earth. But there might still be microbes somewhere nearby. There could have been life on other planets in the past, too. Venus was possibly quite like Earth until 700 million years ago. Could it have had life then? No one knows.

Some of the moons of the gas giants have vast oceans below the surface. Life on Earth stayed in the oceans for billions of years, so perhaps it has done so elsewhere—maybe somewhere like Enceladus, a moon of Saturn.

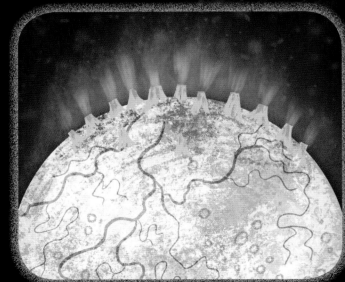

**Enceladus**, with ice volcanoes—a possible place for life in our solar system.

We can spot **exoplanets**—a star dims as a planet crosses it.

exoplanets

## Far, far away

Planets around other stars are called "exoplanets." A tell-tale sign of an exoplanet is a star briefly dimming as a planet passes in front of it. Astronomers work out the size of the exoplanet, how far it is from its star, and whether it might be rocky or gassy. If a planet is warm enough for water to be liquid, it might possibly have life.

Voyager 1

## Looking out for alien life

Although stars naturally produce radio waves, the type of radio waves that we send out from Earth are very different. If living things on another planet also had technology, they might produce similar radio signals that we could pick up and recognize. Any distant aliens with radio telescopes might spot Earth this way, too.

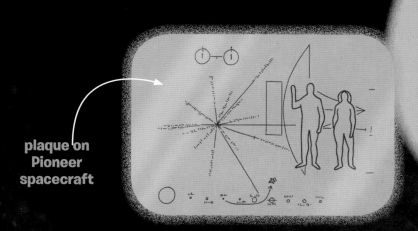

plaque on Pioneer spacecraft

## MESSAGES IN SPACE-BOTTLES

Four spacecraft have set out for distant space carrying messages for any aliens that might find them. Each craft carries an engraved plate showing where it came from. The farthest, Voyager 1, is already outside the solar system and could keep going for billions of years. The two Voyager craft carry special "golden records" (and a player!) holding messages and images of Earth.

# A FUTURE IN SPACE

**Humans have begun to explore space, but there is far more to do. Scientists hope that our adventures in space will uncover more and more information about how the solar system and universe formed, and what other parts of the galaxy and universe are like.**

## Stopping points

Space travel is difficult as it takes a very long time to get anywhere. A return trip to Mars would take about two years, and that's the closest planet we could visit. Plans for a colony on Mars, and a base in space near or on the Moon, aim to provide a hub for longer journeys.

In future, there will be more probes to some of the moons in the solar system to find out if they could host life, and to learn more about conditions in the early solar system.

## OLDER THAN US

Our solar system has existed for only about a quarter the age of the universe. There might be planets much older than ours with intelligent life forms that are millions or billions of years ahead of us with very advanced technology. We only know the story of our own bit of universe, where we are the only known technological beings. There might be truly mind-blowing technologies out there somewhere. They might even be watching us develop.

Energy needs on another planet could be met by using solar panels to capture energy from the Sun.

asteroid mining

## Mine, all mine!

Some organizations are looking at the possibility of trapping space rocks and mining them for valuable minerals and metals. Other experimental work with asteroids aims to divert or destroy any asteroid that looks as though it's heading for a collision with Earth.

If humans were to be able to live on another planet, they'd need to grow food in conditions similar to those on Earth.

## Home from home

Modern life puts a lot of strain on Earth as we use resources, make polluting waste, and raise the temperature, causing climate change. Some people think we might need to start moving to other planets.

It would take a very, very long time (thousands of years) to get to a planet around another star. One possibility might be "terraforming" a nearby planet such as Mars. This means changing a planet or moon to have the conditions we need. It's a huge challenge. Perhaps other civilizations somewhere in the galaxy, or in another galaxy, already have the technology to travel between stars or even adapt planets to suit their own needs.

# ALL GOOD THINGS COME TO AN END

We have learned a great deal about how the universe has come about and grown, and even more about our own solar system. But we don't know what will happen to the universe in the future. We don't even know whether it will ever end or go on forever.

## Going with a bang?
Space scientists have three ideas about the future of the universe:

One possibility is that gravity is strong enough to stop the universe expanding, and pull it all back in toward the middle in a "Big Crunch." This would be a sort of reverse Big Bang. Matter would move together, going faster and faster, until eventually everything is crushed back into a singularity, atoms squashed out of existence. It might then "bounce" back with a new Big Bang, starting a new universe.

Another possibility is that eventually the universe will slowly run out of energy to expand. The universe would run out of gas to make stars, and everything would become more and more similar in a cold, dark, boring universe. This is sometimes called the "Big Freeze."

Or the dark energy forcing the universe apart could keep increasing, making the universe grow and grow until even atoms are torn apart in a "Big Rip."

## Calling time on the Sun
We don't know what will happen to the whole universe (or when it might happen), but we do know the fate of Earth and the Sun. Our Sun will eventually run out of helium to fuse and will turn into a red giant. It will grow larger, finally roasting and destroying Earth as it dies. But don't worry—the Sun is less than halfway through its lifetime, so it's got another five billion years or so to go. By that time, if humans are still around, we will have found other planets to live on. We might have made it to other stars, or even other galaxies. There's a lot of the story of the universe still to be written.

positively curved universe

negatively curved universe

flat universe

## The shape of the universe

Space scientists think the fate of the universe
depends on its shape. If the universe is curved like a ball, it is closed
and will eventually collapse back in on itself in a Big Crunch. If it is flat
or curved like a saddle, its end will be a Big Freeze or a Big Rip.

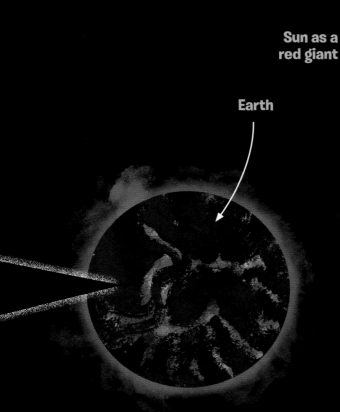

Sun as a
red giant

Earth

# TIMELINE OF THE UNIVERSE

Over billions of years, the universe has grown from an unimaginably tiny point to something unknowably vast. From our place in it, we know it is at least 93 billion light years across, but it could be far larger.

electron

neutron

Scientists don't know what the universe was like before the first $1/10^{32}$ of a second. But by the end of that brief instant, a tiny universe of pure energy, called the singularity, had sprung from nowhere. It was infinitely hot and infinitely dense.

quarks

As the universe cooled more, quarks that collided began to clump in groups. They formed the **protons** and **neutrons** at the heart of all matter. A proton is the nucleus of a hydrogen atom—so hydrogen was the first element to exist.

Gravity separated from the soup of energy and forces that made up the universe.

**BIG BANG AND COSMIC INFLATION**

The universe immediately began to grow bigger and to change. In less than a billionth of a second, it expanded by $10^{26}$ times, perhaps to the size of a golf ball. It's as if an ant grew to the size of our galaxy instantly! As it grew, it also cooled.

By the end of the first second, **quarks** and **electrons**, the first components of matter, existed. They whizzed round in a super-hot soup or plasma.

proton
(hydrogen nucleus)

| time = $10^{-43}$ seconds temp = $10^{32}$K | time = $10^{-32}$ seconds temp = $10^{26}$K | time = 1 second temp = $10^{10}$K | time = 100 seconds temp = 1,000,000,000K |
|---|---|---|---|

**FIRST SECOND** ⟶ **THREE MINUTES**

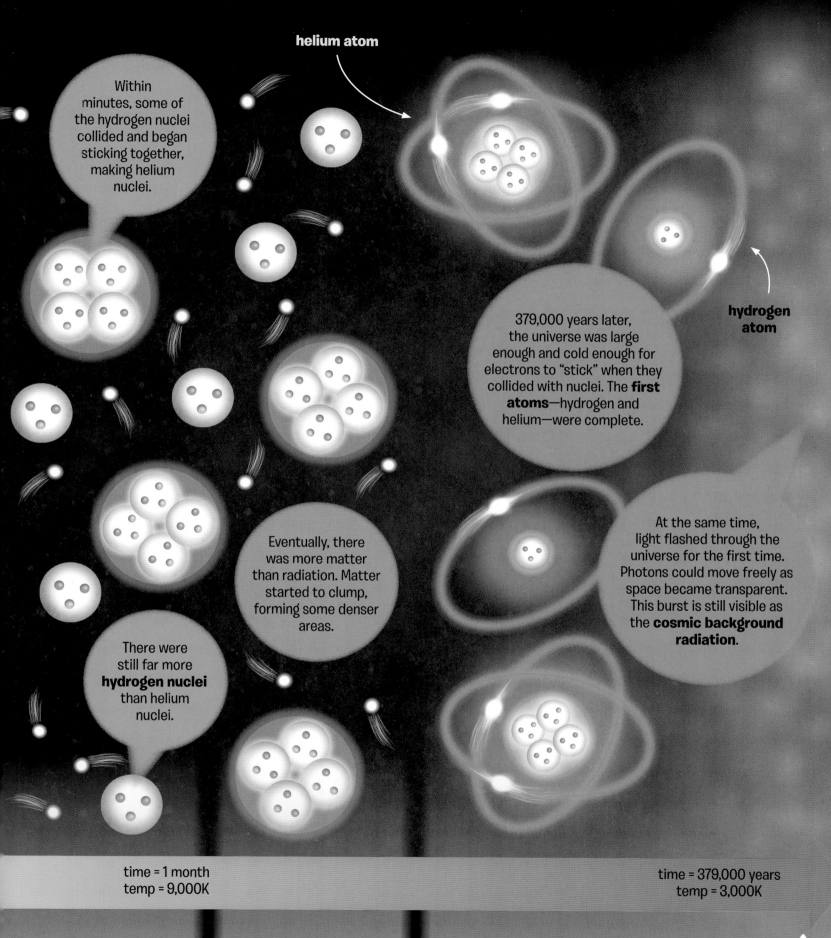

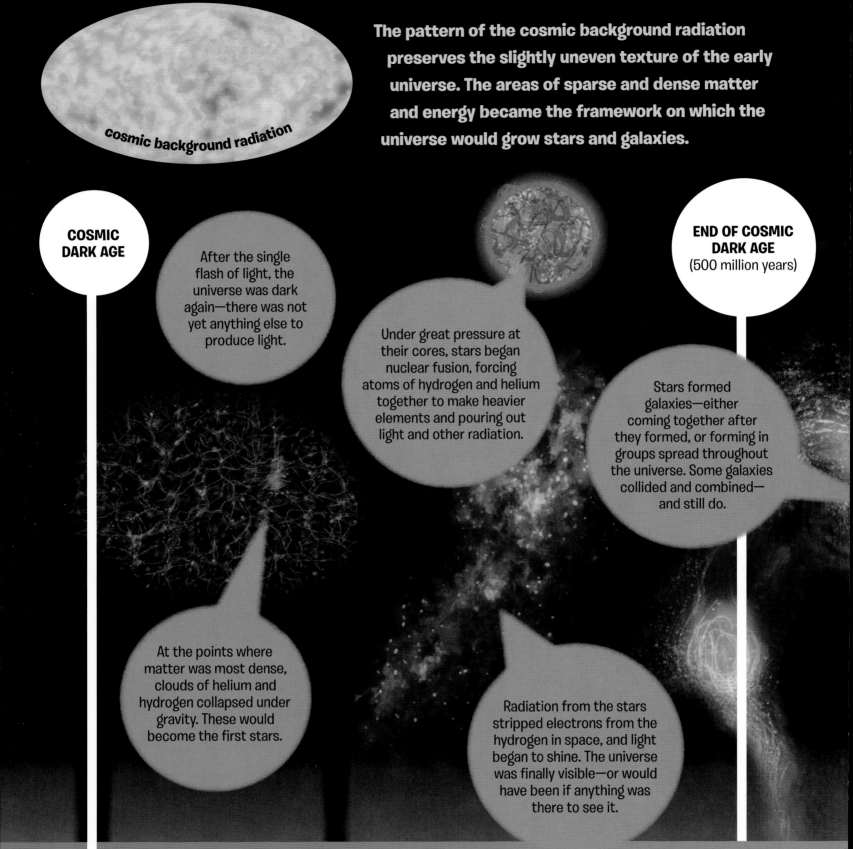

The pattern of the cosmic background radiation preserves the slightly uneven texture of the early universe. The areas of sparse and dense matter and energy became the framework on which the universe would grow stars and galaxies.

cosmic background radiation

**COSMIC DARK AGE**

**END OF COSMIC DARK AGE**
(500 million years)

After the single flash of light, the universe was dark again—there was not yet anything else to produce light.

Under great pressure at their cores, stars began nuclear fusion, forcing atoms of hydrogen and helium together to make heavier elements and pouring out light and other radiation.

Stars formed galaxies—either coming together after they formed, or forming in groups spread throughout the universe. Some galaxies collided and combined—and still do.

At the points where matter was most dense, clouds of helium and hydrogen collapsed under gravity. These would become the first stars.

Radiation from the stars stripped electrons from the hydrogen in space, and light began to shine. The universe was finally visible—or would have been if anything was there to see it.

time = 380,000 years
temp = 3,000K

**380,000 YEARS** ⟶   **100 MILLION YEARS**

The first stars burned brightly and briefly. Then they collapsed in on themselves to make black holes, or perhaps exploded in spectacular supernovas, hurling out more matter into space.

While hydrogen and helium were drawn to the middle of these new stars, heavier matter whirled around them in disks, some already combined as water, minerals, and other substances.

Some of these stars ended their lives in supernovas that scattered the elements they had made into space.

New stars formed in the same way, with matter drawn to points where it was already dense and collapsing until the stars burst into light. Some of these stars were smaller, burned less brightly and for longer. They made heavier elements, up to iron, in their cores.

All the time, the universe was still growing and cooling. Around 5 billion years ago, it began to grow more quickly—dark energy is apparently pushing galaxies further apart.

In the immense energy of a supernova, even heavier elements formed. These, too, were hurled into space.

time = 9 billion years
temp = 5K

**800 MILLION YEARS**

**4 BILLION YEARS**

With a richer mix of matter, the recent universe has been able to make far more than just stars that are balls of gas. Everything on Earth and in the solar system has formed from this mix in the last 4.6 billion years.

The lighter, gassy matter that becomes solid only at very low temperatures formed planets further from the stars.

Mars

The heavier, rocky matter that becomes solid at higher temperatures formed rocky planets nearest the stars.

Jupiter

Stars like our own **Sun** took in most of the matter whirling around them, but there was enough left over to form planets, asteroids, moons, and comets.

Chunks of rock and ice that were not big enough to become planets became the other bodies we see around stars, including **moons** that orbit planets, and **asteroids** and **comets** that orbit the star.

temp = 5K

**4.6 BILLION YEARS AGO**

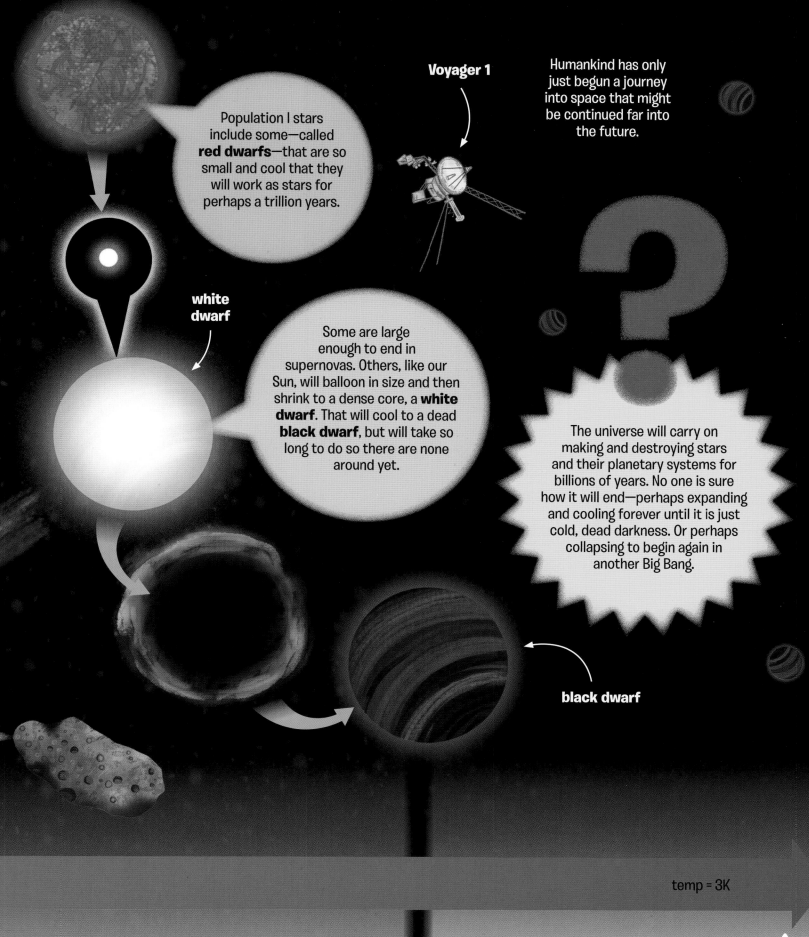

Population I stars include some—called **red dwarfs**—that are so small and cool that they will work as stars for perhaps a trillion years.

**Voyager 1**

Humankind has only just begun a journey into space that might be continued far into the future.

**white dwarf**

Some are large enough to end in supernovas. Others, like our Sun, will balloon in size and then shrink to a dense core, a **white dwarf**. That will cool to a dead **black dwarf**, but will take so long to do so there are none around yet.

The universe will carry on making and destroying stars and their planetary systems for billions of years. No one is sure how it will end—perhaps expanding and cooling forever until it is just cold, dead darkness. Or perhaps collapsing to begin again in another Big Bang.

**black dwarf**

temp = 3K

NOW

... AND BEYOND

# GLOSSARY

**amplitude**  Solid lump of rock and ice that orbits a star but is too small to become a planet.

**asteroid**  Solid lump of rock and ice that orbits a star but is too small to become a planet.

**atmosphere**  Cloak of gases surrounding a planet or other large object in space.

**atom**  The smallest component of matter that can't be divided or separated further. Each chemical element has a different type of atom.

**billion**  A thousand million (1,000,000,000).

**black hole**  Extremely dense object with such intense gravity not even light can escape from it.

**comet**  Lump of ice and rock dust that produces a glowing tail of gas and dust as it approaches the Sun as some of the ice melts and streams away from it.

**condense**  Turn from a gas to a liquid on cooling.

**conductor (of heat or electricity)**  Able to carry heat or electricity.

**constellation**  Pattern of stars in the sky in which people see figures or other pictures.

**cosmic microwave background radiation (CMBR)**  Left-over radiation from the Big Bang, found everywhere throughout the universe.

**dark energy**  Mysterious force that pushes objects in the universe further apart.

**dark matter**  Mysterious matter that accounts for "missing" mass in the universe.

**dense**  With a high concentration of matter in a small space.

**earthquake**  Shaking, juddering, and lurching of the ground that happens when tectonic plates move alongside each other.

**eclipse**  Total or partial darkening of the Sun or another star when a planet or moon moves across its face (so the object moves between us and the Sun or star).

**electromagnetic radiation**  Energy transmitted as waves, including radio, X-rays, microwaves, and visible light.

**electron**  Tiny package of electrical charge that whizzes around the nucleus of an atom.

**element**  One of the 118 fundamental chemicals from which all other substances are built up; each element has a unique type of atom.

**engraved**  With a design cut into the surface.

**filament**  Thin strand.

**flyby**  Journey of a spacecraft going past, but not landing on, a planet or other object in space.

**fossil**  Part or trace of an organism preserved in stone.

**galaxy**  Huge collection of stars held in a group by gravity.

**hemisphere**  Half of a sphere, particularly of Earth (north and south hemispheres).

**infinite**  Without limit.

**Kelvin**  A temperature scale with intervals that correspond to the Celsius scale. On the Kelvin scale, zero degrees (written 0 K) is equal to −273.15°C.

**Kuiper Belt**  Vast cloud of icy lumps around the solar system, beyond the orbit of Neptune.

**lava** Hot, molten rock from Earth's interior (magma) coming from a volcano.

**lichen** Algae and fungi working together, acting like a single organism.

**light year** Unit of distance used in measuring space equal to 9.5 trillion km (6 trillion miles).

**magma** Hot, semi-molten rock that forms the mantle of Earth, below the crust.

**mantle** Thick layer of slow-moving, hot rock below Earth's crust and above its core.

**massive** With a lot of mass.

**meteorite** Lump of rock from space that has landed on Earth.

**microbe** Organism too small to see with the naked eye but visible with a microscope.

**migrating** Moving from one place to another; some animals migrate when the weather changes or to follow seasonal food supplies.

**molecule** Group of atoms bound together.

**neutron** Particle in nucleus of an atom that has no electrical charge.

**nucleus** Middle of an atom, containing protons and neutrons.

**photon** Tiny packet of energy of a particular wavelength.

**photosynthesis** Process by which plants make sugars from carbon dioxide from the air and water, using energy from sunlight.

**protostar** Dense ball of hot, glowing gas that will become a star but has not yet started nuclear fusion.

**proton** Positively charged particle in the nucleus of an atom.

**protoplanet** Chunk of matter that has collected in the disk of gas and dust around a star and has grown to a considerable size but is not yet a planet.

**quark** Smallest component of protons and neutrons, the particles that make up the nucleus of an atom.

**radiation** Energy transmitted as waves or particles (photons).

**satellite** Object that is in orbit around a planet or other object in space; moons are natural satellites.

**singularity** Infinitely small and dense point where matter is super-concentrated.

**solar nebula** Cloud of dust and gas that surrounded the early Sun and from which it formed.

**supernova** Explosion that happens when a star that has used up all the material it can fuse collapses in on itself and then hurls its matter out into space.

**tectonic plate** One of the slabs of Earth's crust that carry the land and oceans.

**trillion** A million million (1,000,000,000,000).

**volcano** Mountain or split in Earth's crust through which hot gases and molten rock ooze or explode.

**wavelength** The distance between peaks of the waves in any form of energy that travels as waves.

# INDEX